# PLACES OF PICASSO

This book is part of
THE BIOGRAPHICAL GUIDE SERIES

*Future titles include*

Artists in Light:
A Biographical Guide to Southern France

Lives in Spain:
A Biographical Guide to Artists and Writers

Pioneering Painters:
A Biographical Guide to Personal Places Plus Paris

# PLACES
*of*
# PICASSO

*A Biographical Guide to Spain and France*

Marilyn Zolton
*and*
Raymond Zolton

Raymar Associates · Bethlehem, N.H.

1998

ISBN 0–9663921–0–9

Library of Congress Catalog Card Number: 98-2754

*Published by:*
Raymar Associates
P.O. Box 62
Bethlehem, NH  03574
raymar@ncia.net

*Printed by:*
Sherwin Dodge Printers
Littleton, NH

*When I was a child, my mother said to me,*
*"If you become a soldier,*
*you'll be a general.*
*If you become a monk,*
*you'll end up as the Pope."*
*Instead, I became a painter and wound up as Picasso.*

—PABLO PICASSO

# Contents

# Introduction

SPAIN AND FRANCE offer visitors many wonderful sights. These range from Greek and Roman remains through centuries of religious and royal architecture to the modern structures of today. There is also a multitude of natural marvels. Many excellent guide books to these sights already exist and it is our intention to supplement them, not to replace them. All tourists will marvel at the Alhambra in Granada or the splendor of the Eiffel Tower; but there are also many individual preferences. Some may thrill to the gore of a bullfight or the glow of an Atlantic sunset while others may prefer the ring of the cash register in the fine shops of Madrid or Paris. For some, though, it may be just as exciting to stand in a room where Cervantes wrote or where Vincent van Gogh died or to see the font at which Picasso was baptized. During many personal trips to Europe, the authors got much enjoyment from visiting sites associated with the lives of prominent artists and writers. Sometimes we found out about these places in various guidebooks, but usually we happened upon them serendipitously. These sites were sometimes in small cities or towns not covered in the guides or the standard information sent by the national tourist offices, but often they were even in the major cities where tourists usually go. How disappointed we would have been to have found out about one of these interesting places after returning home; especially if we had been close by but didn't know about it. We began to scour multiple guides to the same country and found that many such places are haphazardly included in one or another guide but we were disappointed that no specific guide was available to access these sites by person. But how many busy trip-planners have time for such extensive research? Why weren't these facts more easily accessible? Why couldn't we look up our favorite artists or writers somewhere and find out about all the places to go in a country without expending such time-consuming effort? One day, while walking on Cape Cod, we decided that when we retired we would try to produce some books which would serve this purpose.

In the late 1980s we gave up our professional careers as a research scientist and a librarian in demanding corporate positions and decided to focus future trips on researching guidebooks that would have met our earlier needs. During the last ten years we have spent over thirty months traveling in Europe, driving tens of thousands of miles among cities and towns of all sizes. We were convinced that we were not the only people interested in such sites and that such a reference book would satisfy a specific need for scholars and others planning a European trip, especially if their time was limited. The comments of many people we have spoken to about our idea have confirmed this belief.

This book presents information on almost three hundred sites in Spain and France relating to the life of Pablo Picasso. Our information came not only from numerous travel guides but also from comprehensive biographies and innumerable miscellaneous works, many acquired from private sources during our travels. After combing these materials, we traveled extensively throughout Spain and France to verify the present status of the sites identified. These journeys were important for several reasons: lack of specificity in many of the sources; various ages of the sources; and the constant march of development. In actuality, we found many items to be quite different from the written sources and often difficult to locate. This on-site exploration has allowed us to include directions to many of the less accessible sites and we hope that our work abroad makes the reader's experience considerably easier.

The book is divided into two parts: Spain and France. Each country has four chapters which cover various regions. The sites are located in over forty cities and, within each chapter, these are arranged in the sequence of their relationship to Picasso's life. Where there are several sites within one city, these are also arranged chronologically. Sites which are essentially gone are indicated with a diamond symbol in the margin. Those of extraordinary interest are similarly marked with a star. The sites and their addresses have been listed in Spanish, French or Catalan in order to correspond with local maps and signs.

By using this guide one can now travel in Spain and France and find many associations to the life of this interesting artist including the sites of his birth, death, residences and studios, important exhibits and various social events. Regarding museums, we have included only those whose collections include works that we felt were of particular biographical significance. We have chosen not to include the many other museums throughout the two countries which have works by him. Despite his long absence from his native Spain, Picasso remained culturally tied to that country, particularly the province of Catalonia. In this book we will describe numerous Spanish sites connected with the first twenty years of his life and his later trips to Spain. The Spaniards are very proud of this native son and his works are given places of honor in major museums throughout the country. Because most of his life was spent in France one can also find many related places there, especially in Paris and on the Côte d'Azur. We hope our descriptions of these places will be interesting to those who can seek them out and also to those who will only see them in their imaginations.

Finally, we would like to acknowledge the assistance that we received from numerous Spanish and French scholars and archivists who shared with us their knowledge of Picasso's relationships with their localities. In particular we must mention the staff of the Pablo Ruiz Picasso Foundation in Málaga, journalist Angel Padin in La Coruña and Roseline Hierholtz and Mr. and Mrs. David Gilbert in Fontainebleau.

# Biographical Summary

Pablo Ruiz Picasso is considered the foremost figure of 20th-century art. His prolific career was broad in both time and character, spanning more than eighty years and involving media such as painting, graphics, collage, sculpture and ceramics. His work also spanned the entire spectrum of art styles, from his early realism through cubism and on to abstraction. His seminal period was spent in his native Spain but he lived most of his life in France and almost fifty of these years in Paris. The final third of his life was spent in the South of France which reminded him of the Catalan region of northeastern Spain.

Picasso was born dead on October 25, 1881, in the Andalusian coastal city of Málaga; his uncle, the assisting doctor, blew cigar smoke into his nostrils and this miraculously revived the infant. He grew up with an unreasonable fear of illness and premature death which he retained throughout his ninety-one-year life! His father, Don José Ruiz Blasco, was a painter and teacher of art and from a very early age Pablo showed little interest in learning anything not related to that subject. As a child, his father taught him to draw and took him to various places in the city to find interesting subjects for this activity. One of these places was the arena in Málaga where Pablo and his father, the only males in an extended family, frequently attended the bullfights which became a lifelong passion of the boy. Another permanent attachment formed at this time was with the pigeons that his father raised and used as models for drawings and paintings. Picasso often used these as a motif for later works and even named one of his daughters "Paloma," the Spanish word for pigeon. When Pablo was nine years old his father took a teaching position in far-off Galicia and the Ruiz family sailed around to the northwest coast of Spain in the summer of 1891.

They lived in La Coruña from 1891 to 1895 and here, though much younger than the other students, Pablo studied for three years at the art school where his father taught. This exposed him to the artistic ideas of mentors other than his father and led to his decision to devote his life to artistic creation. It was here, at age thirteen, that he had the first public exhibit of his work. Despite the opinion of some biographers that these years were a totally negative experience for him because of the inclement weather and foreign language found here, others claim that this was an important period in the insemination of his artistic development. His father, long dissatisfied with the lack of acceptance of his own work by the local critics, finally took a post in Barcelona in 1895 after the untimely death of Pablo's younger sister.

As in La Coruña his father's influence and Pablo's own ability to pass an entrance test led to his acceptance, at age fourteen, into the Fine Arts Academy of Barcelona. His artistic maturation here was supplemented by his exposure to the political turmoil which was present in this cosmopolitan metropolis. His time outside the Academy was spent mainly in drawing various sites throughout the city and associating with modern artists and anarchists in the cafés. In 1897, on his father's advice, he left his family for the first time to study at the prestigious San Fernando Academy in Madrid, but after two unhappy years he returned to Barcelona. His health was quite poor from having not eaten properly in Madrid and he spent a summer with a friend's family in a Catalan mountain village to regain his strength. This was his first experience of non-city life and it was to make a lasting impression on him. When he returned to Barcelona he lived independently and again began frequently meeting with other young artists in cafés such as the famous 4 Cats, which was named for the Parisian café, Le Chat Noir. Picasso had an exhibit of his work here in early 1900.

The estrangement of his artistic ideals and those of his father became irreconcilable and at the age of nineteen he made his first attempt at life in Paris, which he considered to be the center of the art world. For almost four years he alternated between periods of struggle in Paris and periods of recuperation in Spain. In 1901, after dissatisfaction with how he had been treated by the Ruiz family during the previous Christmas visit to Málaga, Pablo made the unusual decision to use his mother's family name on his work. (Interestingly, this was also done almost three hundred years before by another great Spanish painter, Diego Rodríguez de Silva y Velázquez!) In 1904 he was finally successful enough to make Paris his permanent home.

When he first came to the French capital around 1900 he was a young man who painted in a realistic manner. However, the avant-garde works that he saw in Paris gave him the foundation with which to create his own unique styles. Coming at the end of the artistic revolution which had finally won some acceptance for innovation from the critics and the public, Picasso was able to enjoy much greater financial success than his impressionist and post-impressionist predecessors. After a series of mistresses, in 1918 he married Russian ballerina, Olga Koklova, and moved from the Bohemian neighborhoods to more bourgeois surroundings. From the 1920s onward Picasso was successful enough to indulge his wife's inclination to stay at the posh hotels on the Côte d'Azur. As their marriage became troubled he often would have a satellite abode for himself and a mistress in a nearby village. He fathered one child during this first marriage which ended in divorce in 1935. With two of his subsequent series of mistresses he had three more children. These years were the beginning of his association with a great number of small southern French towns and would eventually lead to his living in the Midi for his last three decades.

Unlike the earlier artists who came to the South for the light and landscapes, Picasso was drawn to this place because he viewed it as an extension of his beloved Catalonia. Throughout his life he associated with many other Catalan expatriates in France and until the Civil War and Franco's domination of his country he made frequent visits back to Spain. In 1934 he made an extended tour through Spain and attended many bullfights; he later tried to promote this sport in southern France. Because of his strong opposition to Franco's policies, Picasso vowed never to set foot in Spain while he ruled; he kept this vow. Even his appointment as director of the Prado Museum in 1936 was carried out totally *in absentia*. In 1937, after the German bombardment of the unarmed population of Guernica, Picasso painted his powerful masterpiece of that name depicting the horror of war and fascism. This large painting was exhibited at the Spanish pavilion of the Paris World Fair in 1937. The advent of this painting to Spain in 1981, after over forty years in the United States, can be considered part of the healing process that took place in the country after the death of Franco. The work now has a place of honor in Madrid's new Queen Sofía Art Center.

Because he spent more than half of his long life there, Picasso's career is inextricably linked to the city of Paris. He was involved, directly or indirectly, in virtually every artistic movement there during the first half of this century. Unlike many artists, Picasso remained in occupied Paris during World War II. At the end of the war he began to live in the South of France and visit Paris, instead of vice versa, although he retained an apartment in the capital until about 1967. In the mid-1940s he lived in several towns on the Côte d'Azur, most notably spending over a year living and working in the castle at Antibes. In 1946 he began his long association with the Madoura Pottery studio in Vallauris, where he would create ceramics for the next twenty-five years. Here he met a young woman named Jacqueline Roque, whom he married in 1961, at age seventy-nine. The immense financial success of his career enabled Picasso to spend the last decades of his life in various villas in the surrounding area and throughout this period he devoted much time to his work in ceramics. He died in Mougins in 1973 and is buried in view of Cezanne's beloved Mount Sainte-Victoire at Vauvenargues, near Aix-en-Provence, in the garden of one of the castles that he had bought during these affluent years.

# Part I

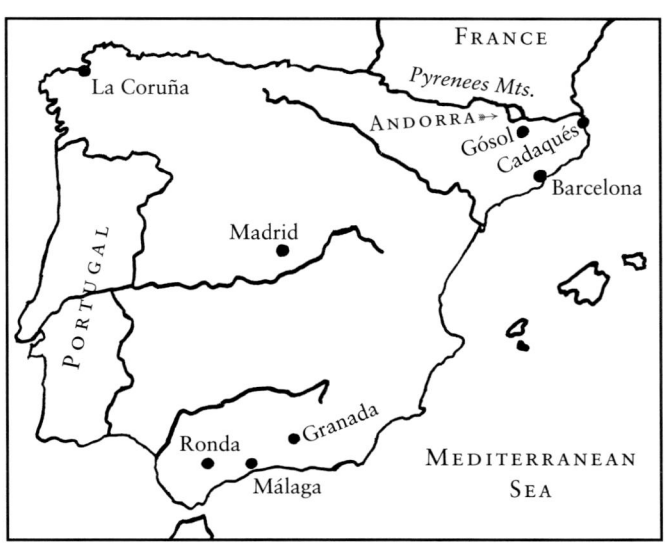

# SPAIN

*Picasso's birthplace, 15 Plaza de Merced, Málaga*

# CHAPTER ONE

# *Andalusia*

ANDALUSIA is probably the most stereotypically "Spanish" region. Many of the cultural images of the country derive from there. It is the home of the flamenco dance, bullfighting and Moorish architecture. The region covers the entire southern part of the country and includes the posh Costa del Sol as well as the awesomely high Sierra Nevada mountains.

## *Málaga*

Picasso's first decade was spent in his native Málaga, considered the sunniest city in Europe. Like many other places in Andalusia it was steeped in the influence of almost eight centuries of Moorish rule. Despite its relatively small size at that time, it was second only to Barcelona as a major Spanish seaport. Picasso's early drawings here often depicted two subjects that were to remain dear to his heart throughout his life—bullfighting and the sea. Today, although the city has become a large metropolitan seaside resort, one can still see many of the sites related to Picasso's years here.

### SPECIFIC SITES IN MÁLAGA

★15 **Plaza de Merced.** On October 25, 1881, Picasso was born on the third floor of this house. Today the well-preserved five-story building, with two plaques on the outside, houses the Pablo Ruiz Picasso Foundation which is dedicated to the advancement of modern art. The Foundation sponsors lectures, exhibits and seminars on Picasso's work and other relevant topics. There are here three original works by Picasso: two drawings, "Dreams and Lies of Franco" (1937) and "A Study for Guernica;" and a framed handwritten poem, "On the Horrors of War." There are also many photographs of the artist and his family on display. The public is welcome.

*Church of Santiago El Mayor, Málaga, where Picasso was baptized*

**Iglesia de Santiago El Mayor, Calle de Granada.**    Sixteen days after his birth Picasso was baptized in this 15th-century church which is located very near the Plaza de Merced. The baptismal font may still be seen at the right rear. Also, his parents were married here in 1880.

**Academia de Bellas Artes, 7 Plaza de Constitución.**    Picasso's father, who earned his living as a teacher of art, taught here during the 1880s. At that time it was called the San Telmo School of Arts and Crafts.

**Café de Chinitas, 6 Pasaje Chinitas.** In the 1880s this café was a gathering place for Bohemian artists and was frequented by Picasso's father. It later became a music hall featuring flamenco music and erotic shows and was a popular gathering place for artists and writers. In 1937, during the Civil War, it was closed by order of the city. The building, now a shop, still has the columns of its original facade.

*Location of Café de Chinitas, Málaga*

*Plaza de Toros, Málaga*

✧ **62 Calle La Victoria.**   In December, 1884, during an earthquake, the Ruiz family took shelter here at the home of painter Antonio Muñoz Degrain, a friend of Picasso's father and later a teacher of Pablo. While they were in this house, which was sheltered by the rocks of the Gibralfaro, Picasso's sister Lola was born on Christmas day.

**Mesón de San Rafael, 40 Compañía.**   This 19th-century building was the location of the Colegio de San Rafael, a school which Picasso attended at age six. It was also the home of Joaquín Martínez de la Vega, an artist whom the young Picasso sometimes visited with his father. There is a plaque commemorating the death of Martínez here.

**Plaza de Toros, Paseo de Reding.**   As a child Picasso was often taken here by his father; one of his earliest paintings, at age eight, was of a mounted picador that he had seen. He kept this painting all his life, as well as a love of bullfighting. The arena, built in 1874, is still in use. There is a fine view of the bullring from the heights of the Alcázar.

**Farola, at the end of Paseo de la Farola.**   At age eight, with the help of his father, Picasso did his first painting, "Lighthouse at Málaga." This light-house, which still guards the harbor, was his subject. Two good vantage points for seeing it are the duck pond of the Paseo del Parque and the heights of the 11th-century Alcázar.

**Jardines de Picasso, Avenida de Andalusia.**    This park, named in honor of the artist, is located across the Puente Tetuán from the city center, about a half-mile from the river. The gardens contain two monuments to Picasso, one of which is a large 1976 sculpture by Berrocal.

★ **Museo de Bellas Artes, 6 San Agustín.**    This museum, housed in the former palace of the Counts of Buena Vista, has a room devoted to the works of Picasso. The collection includes two very early paintings done at age fourteen, two drawings done at age nineteen, and numerous items donated by his secretary, Jaime Sabartés, including some autographed books. A nearby room is dedicated to the works of Antonio Muñoz Degrain, a teacher of Picasso. During the 1880s, Picasso's father was the curator of an earlier city art museum and also responsible for the restoration of old paintings there.

**Palacio de Justicia, Paseo Marítimo Pablo Ruiz Picasso.**    Every October, the month of the artist's birth, a festival called "Octobre Picassiano" is held here. The building was formerly the luxurious Hotel Miramar.

## Granada

This historic city was the seat of Islamic rulers after the reconquest of Córdoba in the 13th century. The extensive buildings of the Alhambra, a hill that dominates the city, are reminders of the artistic achievements by this culture at its zenith in the 14th century. The palaces and fortresses of this complex surround courtyards of flowers, trees and fountains. Granada was the last bastion of the Moors who were finally defeated by Queen Isabella and King Ferdinand in 1492, almost eight hundred years after their invasion in 711. One of the composers with whom Picasso collaborated was Manuel de Falla, a native of this Andalusian metropolis. Today his small simple home is the **Museo Manuel de Falla**, at 11 Antequeruela Baja, near the Alhambra woods. The collection contains much memorabilia of his life and among the exhibits are Picasso's set designs for the London premiere of his *The Three-Cornered Hat*. This premiere appropriately took place in the Alhambra Theatre on July 22, 1919.

## Ronda

Ronda is a charming mountain village which sits on the edge of a deep ravine about fifty kilometers west of Málaga. It is home to one of Spain's oldest bullrings. Built in 1785, it was in modern times used in the filming of the opera, *Carmen*. The historic structure borders the ravine and traditionally the dead bulls were disposed of by dumping them directly out of the bullring into the abyss. It is certainly fitting for a lifetime fan of this sport to be honored by the town in the **Alameda del Tajo,** on Calle Virgen de la Paz, a lovely garden which overlooks the ravine near the bullring. Here, located in the far right corner of the park near the mirador, there is a bronze head of Picasso on a stone base. The monument was installed here in 1981 on the centenary of his birth.

*Bust of Picasso in the Alameda del Tajo, Ronda*

# CHAPTER TWO

# *Galicia*

GALICIA IS the region in the northwest corner of Spain, the western-most part of what is called the "Green Coast." The countryside is reminiscent of the rolling green hills of Ireland while the coast is lined with narrow inlets, called *rias*, which resemble the fjords of Norway. The most famous town in the region is the pilgrimage site of Santiago de Compostella.

## *La Coruña*

La Coruña, the capital of Galicia, has long been an important seaport. Its longevity is demonstrated by the presence of a Roman lighthouse at its harbor. It was from here that the "invincible" Spanish Armada sailed to its final battle in 1588, when it was destroyed by the navy of Sir Francis Drake. Picasso spent his years from age nine to thirteen in this northwest outpost; in language and weather it was dramatically different from the Andalusia of his early childhood. His three years at the art school here exposed him to ideas much less provincial than those of his father and by the time he left this city he had had his first public exhibit and had acquired independent ideas on how he would pursue his artistic life. There are many things to see here that relate to Picasso's stay and the surrounding countryside is a unique part of Spain which visitors often bypass. After many years of indifference, there is now an association working towards the establishment of a museum in Picasso's former home which, like several other sites, remains much the same today as it was in his time.

### SPECIFIC SITES IN LA CORUÑA

**14 Calle Payo Gómez.** The second-floor apartment in this building was the home of the Ruiz family during their four years in La Coruña. It was here that Pablo did his early paintings, "The Man with the Cap" and

"The Barefoot Girl," both of which he personally kept until his death and which are now in the Picasso Museum in Paris. Also, his beloved younger sister, Conchita, died here of diphtheria in 1895. Some things about the building remain the same: the second-floor hallway still has the ceiling-high cabinets of which Picasso later spoke and the back balcony, from which his mother was able to watch him at play in the nearby Plaza de Pontevedra, overlooks the patio where he and his father painted the many pigeons that lived there. In 1985, on the 90th anniversary of his first exhibition, the authorities installed on the building a plaque denoting his residence here.

**Instituto Da Guarda, Plaza de Pontevedra.** The lower floor of this Da Guarda building (named for the citizen that paid for its construction) housed the Escuela Provincial de Bellas Artes where Don José Ruiz Blasco obtained a teaching post in 1891. His son Pablo attended the Instituto de La Coruña in the same building for one year. The following year, although only ten years of age and much younger than the other students, the boy began his three-year enrollment in the art school at the special request of his father. In these corridors he fell in love for the first time with Angeles Méndez to whom he gave many drawings of pigeons; she was the subject of his painting "The Barefoot Girl," done when he was thirteen years old. At this school he studied under Isadoro Brocos Gómez who had many dis-

*Instituto Da Guarda, La Coruña, where Picasso's father taught art*

*Picasso Pigeon Sculpture in front of Instituto Da Guarda, La Coruña*

*Torre de Hercules,
Roman lighthouse in
La Coruña*

cussions with the young student about the work of the Spanish masters, El Greco and Goya, and about the new French art movements of the day, especially impressionism. The many classical statues and fragments used as models by Picasso and the other students are still part of the school's ambience, but it has now moved to a new location on **Calle de Orillamar,** where also are preserved the documents related to Picasso's enrollment. The Da Guarda Building, which was built in 1889 and enlarged in 1898, now houses a college. In front of the building, in the lovely Plaza de Pontevedra, is a large white pigeon sculpture by Picasso covered with repeated signatures. This motif was frequently used' by the artist who had drawn pigeons as a boy here with his father. He later named one of his daughters "Paloma," the Spanish word for pigeon.

**Torre de Hercules, at the end of Avenida de Navarre.** This ancient lighthouse was built by the Romans in the 2nd century A.D. It was restored in the 18th century and is still functioning. Picasso did a drawing of it at age ten.

**Playa del Orzán, Calle Juan Canalejo.** Picasso often spent spare time here sunning himself or playing in the water. It remains today an excellent sheltered bathing beach.

✧ **11 Calle Payo Gómez.** The building which occupied this site when Picasso lived here was the home of Dr. Ramón Perez Costales, a close friend of the family from their arrival in La Coruña. Picasso greatly admired this man and frequently visited here; he painted two interior scenes in this home. It was here that he came to summon the doctor when his sister, Conchita, was gravely ill in 1895.

**Iglesia de Santa Lucia, Plaza de Lugo.** This parish church was the location of the funeral of Picasso's sister, Conchita, who died of diphtheria at age seven in January, 1895.

**Cementerio de San Amaro, Calle de Orillamar.** This was the burial place of Picasso's sister, Conchita, in 1895. After some indecision, his father allowed the boy to participate in the funeral cortege. The exact site of her grave is no longer known.

**20 Calle Real.** Picasso's work was exhibited publicly for the first time in the spring of 1895 in this building, which remains the same except that the ground floor was then a furniture store owned by Joaquín de la Torre. His paintings were well received by the local critics who had been consistently harsh on all the works of his father for the previous four years. This contributed to the strained relations developing between the conservative art professor and his gifted son, who was already being influenced by his

*Site of Picasso's first exhibition, 20 Calle Real, La Coruña*

knowledge of the modern art movements in France. It would be but five years until Pablo would seek his own fortune in Paris at age nineteen.

**Museo Provincial de Bellas Artes, Calle de Panaderas.** This museum has a large painting "Vista de La Coruña, 1891" by Alejandro Ferrant which shows the city as it was at the time of the Ruiz family's arrival there.

# CHAPTER THREE

# *Catalonia*

THE REGION of Spain that is called Catalonia is just part of the ancient kingdom that once spanned the high Pyrenees to include some of what is now the Roussillon area of France. Catalonia was a prosperous dominion which even conducted trade with the Far East during the Middle Ages. Today it is the most autonomous Spanish region and the Catalan language prevails as its official tongue. A wealth of past architecture dating from the Greeks and Romans through the romanesque to the gothic leads one to the modern buildings of Antonio Gaudi which adorn the capital of Barcelona.

## *Barcelona*

The last home of the Ruiz family was Spain's second largest city, a major seaport boasting two thousand years of history. As the capital of semi-autonomous Catalonia it offered a unique culture relatively uninfluenced by the short stay of the Moors or even by the dominant Spanish nation. Although the major language was Catalan, Picasso found this city more to his liking than La Coruña had been. He made several lasting friendships here and even during his long stay in France he associated with many Catalan expatriates and often vacationed in Catalonia. Thus it is fitting that the visitor to this charming metropolis can find here a major museum devoted to Picasso as well as numerous sites related to his life.

### SPECIFIC SITES IN BARCELONA

**3 Calle Reina Cristina.**  This was the Ruiz family's first home in Barcelona for a short time in 1895. It is near La Lonja art school where Picasso's father taught. The five-story apartment building is still there on the narrow street.

**Escuela de Bellas Artes de La Lonja, Passeig Isabel II.**  For two years, 1895–1896, Picasso attended this institution where his father was a teacher.

15

Because of his artistic ability he was admitted here at age fourteen, even though the usual age of acceptance was twenty. The school is still in operation in part of the top floor of this large classical building which serves as the Barcelona Stock Exchange. On nearby Carrer Consolat de Mar, Picasso's friend Jaime Sabartés lived in an apartment where the artist decorated the walls for him in 1904.

**4 Calle Llauder.**   Picasso lived here with his family in 1895. The five-story apartment building is still occupied.

**4 Calle de la Plata.**   Biographical sources say that at age fifteen Picasso's father arranged for him to have a studio here. It was here that he did the large painting, "Science and Charity," which won some awards for the young artist. His father modeled for the doctor in the painting. The building still exists but the one opposite, with an art store on the ground floor called "Taller Picasso," claims that the studio was there, at #5.

✧ **12 Carrier Nou de la Rambla.**   Here, on this street formerly named Calle Conde del Asalto, was located the Eden Concert (or Café de la Alegria) where Picasso and other young artists gathered in the mid-1890s.

**Calle Avinyó.**   On this narrow street near the harbor, formerly the red-light district of the city, Picasso lost his virginity in a brothel in 1896, at age 15. An early precursor of his cubist period, "Les Demoiselles d'Avignon," depicted the women here; the painting was done in 1907 but not shown until 1916 in the Salon d'Antin in Paris. Today this masterpiece hangs in the Museum of Modern Art in New York.

**3 Calle de la Merced.**   Picasso lived here with his family on this street near the harbor in 1896–1897. The building is still standing, but the inside has been renovated.

★ **Four Cats Café, Carrer Montsió.**   As a young man in Barcelona Picasso spent much time in this cabaret associating with other artists with an interest in modern art. One of the people he met here was Jaime Sabartés, who became his lifelong friend and secretary and was instrumental in the foundation of the Picasso Museum in Barcelona in 1960 (see below). During this time Picasso designed a colorful menu for the café. In February, 1900, several months before leaving for Paris, he held an exhibit of his work here. The portraits of his friends which were part of this exhibit, along with newspaper reviews of the show, hang today in the back room of the café. The front room has many photos of the Barcelona scene of that era. The site is still an active night spot and eatery reached from Avinguda Portal de L'Angel near Galerias department store.

**1 Calle de Escudilleras Blancs.**   Picasso had a studio here with friends from 1899 to 1900; the ground floor was a corset factory where he en-

*Exterior of 4 Cats Café, Barcelona*

*Interior of 4 Cats Café, Barcelona*

joyed bantering with the young girls who worked there. The five-story stone building still stands with a restaurant now on the ground floor.

**Estación de Francia, Avenida Marqués de L'Argentera.**   From this large classical railroad station, Picasso and his friend Carles Casagemas left Barcelona in the fall of 1900 and traveled third-class to Paris. During the next four years Picasso left Barcelona from here three more times as he struggled to establish himself as an artist in Paris.

**Sala Pares, 5 Petritxol.**   In May, 1901, Picasso held his first major exhibit here during one of his returns from Paris. This Barcelona gallery has been operating since 1840. The **Museum of the City of Barcelona** on Plaza del Rey has a diorama of the salon as it was in the 1880s.

**6 Carrer Nou de la Rambla.**   Picasso lived here in 1902 when the street was called Calle Conde del Asalto. The brothel that was also located here at that time inspired his painting of a madam, "La Celestina," done in Paris in 1904. The five-story building with a carved façade still stands; there is no notation.

**Café Torino.**   Around 1902 Picasso and his friends liked to stroll the Ramblas, an activity that is still popular with the local population as well as the tourists. Here they would play the slot machines at the modern Café Torino, on a corner opposite Placa de Catalunya.

**28 Calle de Comercio.**   In 1904, after several short stays in Paris, Picasso lived here in the former studio of his friend Carles Casagemas who had committed suicide in Paris in 1901. While here he painted his famous blue-period painting, "La Vie," in which the male figure is Casagemas. The five-story stone building still remains but has no notation.

✧ **18 Porta Ferriffa.**   This site, in the old section of the city, was the location of the Dalmau Gallery where Picasso had an exhibit in 1912. The building is now occupied by a shop and the Dalmau Gallery is now located at 349 Consell de Cent.

**Teatro Liceo, 28 Rambla de Capuchinos.**   In 1917, this theater was the venue for a performance of the Jean Cocteau ballet, *Parade*, for which Picasso designed the sets. While working on this project in Paris he had fallen in love with one of the dancers, Olga Koklova, and so followed the show to Barcelona. Here he introduced her to his family and they were later married in Paris. This theater is considered one of Europe's finest concert halls and was still in operation until 1994 when the interior was damaged by fire. It is undergoing major restoration and reopening is planned.

**Paseo de Colón.**   This avenue, with the high monument of Christopher Columbus at its end, was a subject painted on a 1917 visit to Barcelona;

Picasso gave the work to his mother. A ceramic plate depicting this scene is now in the Picasso Museum in Barcelona.

✧ **Galeria Layetanas, 613 Gran Vía de les Corts Catalanes.**   A new bank building today stands on the site of the gallery where the prosperous Picasso received a tribute from old friends in 1918.

**Hotel Ritz, on Gran Vía at Carrer de Roger de Lluria.**   In sharp contrast to the surroundings of his earlier years in Barcelona, Picasso with his wife and son stayed in this five-star hotel on a 1933 visit. Despite widespread economic depression, he was doing very well. The luxurious hotel is still operating.

**Sala Gaspar, 323 Consell de Cent.**   This gallery, which has been in operation since 1909, was the site of a Picasso exhibit in 1956.

**Colegio de Arquitectura, Avinguda de la Catedral and Carrer dels Capellans.**   Picasso was responsible for the decoration of the three outside walls of this building in 1962, at age 81. The three large stone reliefs are

*Hotel Ritz, Barcelona, where Picasso stayed after becoming affluent*

*College of Architecture, Barcelona, with façades designed by Picasso*

above the plate glass of the ground floor. Inside, the exhibition hall is named in his honor.

**Iglesia de San Pablo del Campo, Calle de Sant Pau.**   The corner of the cloister of this church is the subject painted on a ceramic plate in the collection of the Picasso Museum in Barcelona.

**Cinema Basque, Rambla del Prat.**   Of the four sculptures on the façade of this building, Picasso's face is the one on the right. The structure remains intact with a modern theater built into the lower level.

**Museo de Arte de Catalonia y Cerámica, Palacio Nacional de Montjuich.** This museum exhibits an outstanding collection of Catalan art ranging from early gothic and romanesque periods to the present day. The major collection of ceramics on the first floor includes a work by Picasso.

**Museo de Arte Moderno, Parque de la Ciudadela.**   This fine collection includes a 1913 stone sculpture of Picasso's head by Pablo Gargallo. There are also portraits of some of his Barcelona friends, including gallery owner Josep Dalmau and Pere Romeu, the owner of the Four Cats Café.

★**Museo Picasso, 15 Calle de Montcada.**   This museum, located in a 15th-century palace, was established in 1960 through the efforts of Picasso's secretary and lifelong friend, Jaime Sabartés. At the time, Picasso himself wanted the museum located at the former home of the Catalan artist, Ramón Pitxot, which was nearby on the same street. Sabartés used his personal collection of Picasso works, along with items still owned by the artist and his second wife, to create an exhibit emphasizing Picasso's early work, 1890–1904. The collection includes portraits of the artist's father, mother, sister, aunt and dog, as well as several self-portraits; there are also portraits of his friends and associates from Barcelona, including one of Carles Casagemas and two of Sabartés. Examples of some later work include 1957 plates and prints of his "Bullfighting" series and his drawings based on the Velázquez masterpiece, "The Maids of Honor" ("Las Meninas"). There are also drawings of his second wife and some ceramic plates and a vase donated by her.

**Passeig de Picasso.** On this street, outside the Parc de la Ciutadella, is a controversial 1983 sculpture, "Homage to Picasso," by the Catalan artist Antoni Tàpies. The large glass cube, with water pouring down its sides and items of Picasso's within, stands before an ornate iron fence designed by Antonio Gaudi.

## Horta de Sant Joan

Horta de Sant Joan is located in Terra Alta, a small mountainous jurisdiction southwest of Barcelona. The village is about one hundred kilometers southwest of Tarragona. It is an area of small population but has been inhabited since the Iron Age. In 1898, in poor health from not eating properly while in Madrid, Picasso lived and worked for a year in this rural area at the home of a friend's family on **Calle Pintor Ruiz Picasso,** off Plaza de la Iglesia. During this period he greatly enjoyed the time that he and his friend spent camping out in the nearby caves, Els Ports. While regaining his health here, he became enamored of the country life, familiar with the Catalan language, and more confident about himself and his art. He decided to become independent of his family and shortly after returning to Barcelona from here, he made his first trip to Paris. After becoming financially successful, he returned here to spend the summer of 1909 at the town's only inn and amazed the locals by flashing 1000-peseta notes. Today this small mountain village remains essentially the same in appearance, with narrow winding streets, one of which is named after Picasso.

## Sitges

About forty kilometers southwest of Barcelona lies Sitges, a lovely seaside city which was the location of summer homes of many wealthy Catalan families. In 1900 Picasso came here to visit his friend Carles Casagemas at the villa of his mother's family, which overlooked the beach. While here they drank at several taverns and Picasso did a charcoal portrait of Santiago Rusiñol. The former home of this local artist on Calle Fonollar is now the **Museo Cau-Ferrat** whose collection includes four drawings and one painting done by Picasso at age 19–20. Another interesting place to visit in Sitges is the **Restaurante 4 Gats**, at 13 Carrer Sant Pau. This fine restaurant, serving Catalan cuisine, is a recreation of the famous Barcelona café of the same name and has many Picasso prints on its walls. Shortly after Picasso's visit here the two young men made their first trip to Paris and shared an apartment there. In 1901 Casagemas committed suicide in the restaurant next door to their Paris studio; this inspired Picasso's blue-period painting "The Burial."

## Gósol

In 1906 Picasso used the funds from a successful sale of paintings to leave Paris with his first longterm mistress, Fernande Olivier, and visit his beloved Catalonia. They spent the summer in this remote mountain village near the border of Andorra, about one hundred kilometers northwest of Barcelona. The residents there amused them with tales of their primary livelihood, smuggling cattle and tobacco through the mountains to France. Picasso thrived in this environment and his work here was quite different

*View as one enters the town of Gósol*

from what he had been doing in Paris. The figures painted here are often nude or in simply draped garments. One example, which is today at the Cleveland Museum of Art, is "The Harem" in which four poses of Fernande surround a hag. In addition to his productive painting, the stay in Gósol stimulated Picasso's interest in sculpting and some of his works here were put into three-dimensional form when he returned to Paris. One example of this was his large painting, "Woman Combing her Hair," which is in the Kimbell Art Museum in Fort Worth, Texas. His ceramic bust of this figure, now in the Pompidou Center in Paris, was sold to Ambroise Vollard who had ten bronze casts made from it. One of these bronzes is owned by the Hirshhorn Museum and Sculpture Garden in Washington, D.C. Picasso's landscapes of Gósol contain many geometric forms and little color and many believe that his contemplation while here led to his conception of cubism the following year. The couple left this retreat sooner than they had planned because the child of the innkeeper became ill and Picasso was always extremely protective of his own health. Then accessible only by mule, Gósol can now be reached by auto via a spectacularly beautiful mountain road. From Barcelona take the road northwest to Manresa then continue north for about sixty kilometers to Berga. Continue north for approximately twenty kilometers, then turn left onto a small road toward Saldes and Gósol, which is about another thirty kilometers.

### SPECIFIC SITES IN GÓSOL

**Can Tempanada, Placa Major at Carrer Pintor Picasso.** While in Gósol, Picasso and Fernande stayed at this simple inn in the center of the village. The owner of this inn was Josep Fontdevila, a man who was said to have been mean and cantankerous with everyone except Picasso, for whom he modeled. The works depicting him include many drawings and watercolors as well as an oil painting which is now at the Metropolitan Museum of Art in New York and a bronze bust which is at the Hirshhorn. Today the inn is a private house but a plaque denotes Picasso's stay.

**Museo Municipal, Placa Major.** This small museum, open only on weekends, has a Sala Picasso which has reproductions of some paintings by Picasso, including one of those done here.

**Placa Major.** In the center of this quaint square is a recently-done sculpture depicting a woman with two large circular loaves of bread on her head. This was the subject of one of the Picasso paintings done here in 1906. Today the painting, "Woman with Loaves," is in the Philadelphia Museum of Art.

*Interior of Can Tempanada, the inn where Picasso stayed in Gósol*

*Bronze statue in Plaça Major, Gósol,*
*based on Picasso's painting, "Woman with Loaves"*

*Placa Major, Gósol, with inn and museum in background*

## Cadaqués

Picasso occasionally vacationed in this lovely seaside town which is located about eighty kilometers northeast of Barcelona not far from the French border. Once a small fishing village on the wild Costa Brava, Cadaqués was discovered by artists and writers in the early 20th century and now has become a charming resort. The popular Spanish artist Salvador Dalí, native of nearby Figueras, had a home here.

### SPECIFIC SITES IN CADAQUÉS

**11 Passatge Poal.**   During the summer of 1910 Picasso lived here right beside the coast and he later did a cubist-style painting of the coastal rocks at nearby Cap Cresus based on this visit. Today the building houses a gallery.

★**Museo Perrot-Moore, 1 Carrer Vigilant.**   This recently opened museum houses a collection devoted to the life and work of Salvador Dalí. It also has a Sala Picasso with numerous items related to that artist: a reproduction of the 1937 masterpiece, "Guernica," along with forty-two preparatory drawings for the painting; a 1964 Dalí portrait of Picasso; a 1969 Picasso portrait of Dalí; and a wax likeness of Picasso in a sedan

*Perrot-Moore Museum, Cadaqués*

*View of Cadaqués*

chair. There are also several items related to Picasso's love of bullfighting: his "Tauromaquia" series of lithographs; two ceramic plates depicting bullfighting scenes; and two 4-meter high paintings of bulls from the set decorations he did for Federico García Lorca's "The Lament for Ignacio Sánchez Mejías" along with a photograph of Picasso with a poster for the 1953 Paris production.

## Figueras

This city of northeastern Catalonia, about eighty kilometers northeast of Barcelona, has two important native sons. One, Narciso Monturiol, was the inventor of the submarine; the other was the flamboyant 20th-century artist Salvador Dalí. The **Teatro-Museo Dalí**, on Plaza Gala i Salvador Dalí, is the second most visited museum in Spain, after the Prado in Madrid. Its comprehensive collection of Dalí's works includes his 1947 surrealistic portrait of Pablo Picasso.

## Serra de Montserrat

This breathtaking mountaintop site, about forty kilometers northwest of Barcelona, is the location of a Benedictine monastery which has existed here since the 9th century. It is a primary destination for pilgrims because of the presence of the "Black Madonna," a 12th-century polychrome wood statue of the Virgin Mary and Infant which was found by a shepherd in a nearby cave. It is also the home of one of Europe's oldest boys choirs, dating back to the 13th century. The monastery operates two museums to display its collections of ancient and modern art. The exhibit of the **Museo de Arte Moderno** includes two remarkable early oil paintings done by Picasso at age 14–15. These are "The Old Fisherman," with his father as the model, and "The Altar Boy." There is also a crayon drawing "The Sardana of Peace" with a description of his donation to this museum in 1961.

# CHAPTER FOUR

# *Madrid and Its Environs*

MADRID, which is at the geographical center of Spain, only became the capital of the country in the 16th century. Previously the Royal Court had moved among several ancient cities such as Valladolid and Toledo. Despite this status, Madrid remained fairly small until the 19th century, but since that time it has grown into a major modern metropolis. At an altitude of 2,120 feet, it is the highest of all European capitals. Picasso spent some time here as a youthful student at the art academy. At that time he became very interested in the city's outstanding art collection in the Prado of which he would ironically be appointed director forty years later. It was an ardent desire of his to have his work hang there some day.

### SPECIFIC SITES IN MADRID

**Real Academia de San Fernando, 13 Calle Alcalá.**   In 1897, financed by his uncle, the 16-year-old Picasso attended this academy to study art. He was accepted after passing a difficult entrance exam but was extremely unhappy here and left after only one year, having benefited mainly from viewing the academy's collection of masterpieces, especially those of Goya. Today the museum of this still-operating academy has several items related to Picasso. One is a display of thirty-one engravings from the "Le Gado Guitarte" collection. Another is a medallion commemorating the centenary of his birth in 1981. Finally, there is a drawing by him of "The Frugal Meal;" this is particularly appropriate because his uncle's contribution to his education did not include enough for him to eat properly while here.

**Parque del Retiro, Plaza de la Independencia.**   While in Madrid to study art in 1897, Picasso spent much time sketching in this large park. The beautiful pool in the park was the subject painted on an 1898 ceramic plate now in the Picasso Museum in Barcelona.

**Museo del Prado, Plaza del Prado.**  During 1897, while supposedly studying art at the San Fernando Academy, Picasso spent most of his time at this museum admiring the magnificent works of El Greco, Goya and Velázquez. In 1936, while living in France, he was made Director of the Museum, *in absentia*. During this time of civil war the works had been removed and Picasso had commented that he was director of "an empty museum."

**4 Calle Caballero de Gracia.**  This 5-story building, where Picasso lived briefly in a boarding house in 1901, is still standing today in Madrid's redlight district.

✧**28 Calle Zurbano.**  Picasso moved here in 1901 with a lease for a year. While here, he and Francisco de Assis Soler, a writer-friend from the Four Cats Café, produced a short-lived art and literary journal in the Catalan language entitled, *Arte Joven (Young Art)*. The failure of this journal, along with severe financial problems, caused him to return to Barcelona after only five months. The building has since been replaced by another.

✧**Café de Fornos, 21 Calle Alcalá.**  In 1903 Picasso did a drawing of this café which no longer exists; the site is now occupied by a new bank building. Next door, at #19, the Hotel Regina has in the lobby a photo of the street in 1919.

**Las Ventas, 237 Calle Alcalá.**  In 1934, on a trip through Spain with his new mistress, Marie-Thérèse Walter, Picasso attended bullfights here. During this period his work was emphasizing the themes of the Minotaur and bullfighting. This bullring is still in operation and today there is an adjacent museum devoted to the sport of bullfighting.

**Casón de Buen Retiro, 28 Calle Alfonso XII.**  In 1937 Picasso painted his masterpiece, "Guernica," for the Spanish Pavilion of the Paris World Fair. Although the work was based on the Germans' massive aerial bombing of this northern Spanish city in which two thousand people were killed in three hours, Picasso intended it as an example of the horrors of all modern warfare. After forty-two years in a New York museum, the work was returned to Spain after the death of Franco and hung in this annex of the Prado, one of only two remaining parts of the 17th-century palace of Philip IV which was decorated by Diego Velázquez. In addition to the painting itself, the exhibit included many photos, sketches, etc. related to its creation and original exhibition in Paris. Because of his lifelong wish to have his work hang in the Prado, Picasso's will stipulated that this painting be given to Spain only if hung there. This annex was seen as meeting this requirement, but in 1991 "Guernica" was moved to a new museum of Spanish modern art despite legal protests on behalf of the Picasso estate. Thus Picasso is no longer represented in the Prado; the Casón de Buen Retiro now houses other works from the museum's huge collection.

*Entrance to the Prado Museum, Madrid*

★ **Centro de Arte Reina Sofía, 52 Calle Santa Isabel.** This new museum is housed in a restored former hospital. Its collection attempts to show the major impact of Spaniards on 20th-century art and thus includes many works by Picasso. A special alcove has become the new home for the most important of these, his 1937 masterpiece, "Guernica," which depicts the horror of the German bombardment of a peaceful Basque town during the Spanish Civil War. There are also more than forty preparatory drawings for this painting as well as some paintings called "Postscripts to Guernica." In addition, one can find the following paintings which span the lifetime of Picasso's career: "The Lady in Blue" (1901); the large "Musical Instruments on a Table" (1925); "Still Life (1944); "Monument to the Spaniards Who Died for France" (1946–1947); and three versions of "Painter and a Model" (1963). Representing Picasso's sculpture is a six-foot bronze, "The Offering Woman," done in 1933. Finally, there is a terra cotta head of Picasso done in 1913 by Pablo Gargallo.

**Museo Thyssen-Bornemisza, 8 Paseo del Prado.** This wonderful private collection, which was formerly in Lugano, Switzerland, is now on loan to Spain. Here it is housed in a restored palace and is open to the public on a regular museum schedule. The collection includes the following paintings by Picasso: "Harvesters" (1907); a small still life, "Glasses and Fruit" (1908); "Man with Clarinet" (1911–1912); "Head of a Man" (1913–1914); and "Harlequin with a Mirror" (1923).

## Buitrago del Lozoya

This town is located on highway N-1 about seventy-five kilometers north of Madrid. The **Museo Picasso**, on Plaza Picasso, is signposted from the highway. This small but interesting museum, open since 1985, contains the collection of personal gifts from Picasso to Eugenio Arias, his former barber. The items on display include the following: numerous drawings, inscribed and signed by Picasso; many books on Picasso's art, autographed by him; some ceramic plates and two barber basins decorated by the artist; a wooden case of barber tools with cover decorated and signed by Picasso in 1960; and a bronze sculpture of Picasso's head done in 1960 by F. Augilar.

# Part II

ENGLISH CHANNEL

Gisors

Paris

Dinard

Le Tremblay

Fontainebleau

ATLANTIC OCEAN

Royan

PROVENCE

Biarritz

Cannes

Perpignan

SPAIN

Pyrenees Mts.

MEDITERRANEAN SEA

# FRANCE

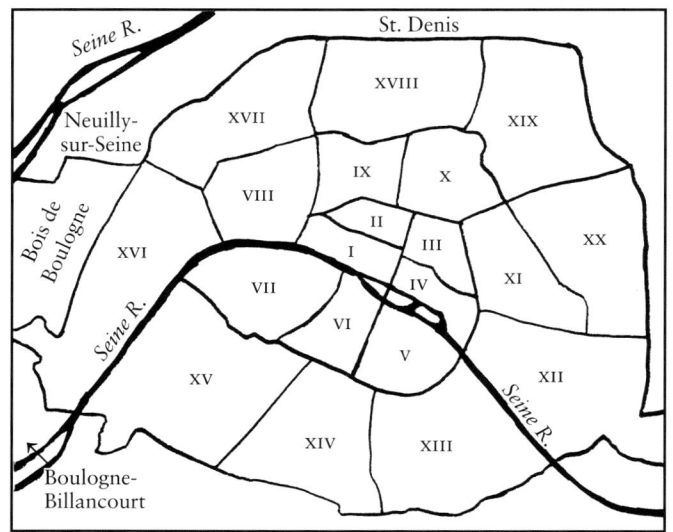

*Paris and its arrondissements*

# CHAPTER FIVE

# Paris
# and Its Environs

Paris is an ancient city that was first settled in the 3rd century B.C. It later became an important Roman outpost known as Lutetia. The original city was on the Ile de la Cité, an island in the Seine River where Notre-Dame cathedral now stands. The name Paris dates from 360 A.D. and since that time the city has been the most important in France. Today it is a modern metropolis that is graced with many wide boulevards that were built in the 19th century by Baron Haussmann. Many old churches and buildings still exist among the archetypical apartment houses that line its streets. Most of the city center remains remarkably free of skyscrapers, giving it a charm unlike other great cities. It has long been considered the center of the art world and the young Picasso, like many other artists, came here to make his place in that world. Places connected with his life and work are to be found throughout the city, from the butte of Montmartre in the north to the southern neighborhood of Montparnasse. In addition, since 1985 one can visit an entire museum devoted to him in the restored 17th-century Hôtel Salé in the historic Marais district. Paris is divided into twenty districts called *arrondissements*. The Seine flows through the heart of the city with six of these districts (Vth, VIth, VIIth, XIIIth, XIVth and XVth) on its Left Bank and the remaining fourteen on its Right Bank. Each of the sites below is followed by the number of its *arrondissement*.

### SPECIFIC SITES IN PARIS

**Musée d'Orsay, 1 Rue de Bellechasse (VII)**   Before being beautifully renovated into a museum, this immense structure was one of the city's major railway stations. This depot, which served trains traveling south to Spain, was Picasso's arrival place early in this century whenever he came to Paris from his home country. In 1935, when his affairs were in turmoil after his divorce, he met here his Spanish friend Jaime Sabartés whom he had invited to come from Barcelona to work as his private secretary. This relationship remained in place for many years and Sabartés was largely responsible for the creation of the Picasso Museum in Barcelona in the 1960s. Today, the Musée d'Orsay has one particular work that Picasso greatly admired: "The Snake Charmer" (1907) by Henri Rousseau.

**9 Rue Campagne-Première** (XIV)   When the young Picasso made his first trip to Paris in October, 1900, he stayed here briefly with his fellow-painter Carles Casagemas. At that time it was the Hôtel du Nouvel Hippodrome.

**49 Rue Gabrielle** (XVIII)   Shortly after arriving in Paris in 1900, Picasso and his artist friends, Carles Casagemas and Manuel Pallarés, rented space

*49 Rue Gabrielle, site of Picasso's first Paris studio*

here. They took over the studio of two other Spanish painters, Isidro Nonell and Ricard Canals, in this section of Montmartre which was at that time a Spanish ghetto. The previous occupants left behind three French girlfriends—Antoinette Fornerod, who became Pallarés' lover; Germaine Gargallo, with whom Casagemas became infatuated; and Odette Lenoir, with whom Picasso became involved. A Picasso drawing, "Leaving the Exposition Universelle, 1900," shows most of these people as well as another Catalan friend, artist Ramon Pichot, who was an intimate of Picasso until he left Paris in 1920. At the Rue Gabrielle studio Picasso celebrated his nineteenth birthday on October 25, 1900. Today a plaque commemorates the building as the site of Picasso's first Paris studio.

**Le Louvre, Cour Napoléon** (I)    As soon as he was settled in Paris in 1900 the young Picasso went immediately to this national museum to view the masterpieces of the collection, just as he had visited the Prado while studying in Madrid. In 1946, in appreciation of Picasso's donation of a series of paintings to the French government, his paintings were hung in one of the Louvre's galleries beside the works of the old masters. Picasso was thrilled with seeing this juxtaposition. In 1971, in honor of his ninetieth birthday, this museum, which normally does not display modern art, set up a special exhibit of eight of his works. At this time, because of his age, the artist was represented at the opening ceremony by his son.

**Grand Palais, Avenue Winston-Churchill** (VIII)    This palace was newly built for the 1900 International Exposition. Picasso, only shortly after arriving in Paris, managed to have one of his paintings, "Last Moments," displayed in the Spanish section of the art exhibition. When Picasso came to see this exhibition he saw more recent works than those in the Louvre. Here he was introduced to the paintings of Éduard Manet, Edgar Degas, Claude Monet, Camille Pissarro, Paul Cézanne, Pierre-Auguste Renoir and Georges Seurat. These were the innovators of the recent past who had paved the way for his own brilliant career to come. In 1907, shortly after Cézanne's death, Picasso was able to see a large number of his works exhibited here at the Salon d'Automne. Picasso considered Cézanne as his greatest master and a father to all modern artists. At this same Salon d'Automne in 1944, just after the liberation of Paris from German occupation, Picasso himself was honored with an entire room to exhibit his works. This palace was the venue for another large Picasso exhibit staged to celebrate the artist's eighty-fifth birthday in 1966; this show, the first after the palace had been renovated, was attended by over 850,000 people. Six years after his death, in 1979, over eight hundred Picasso works were displayed here for three months; these works would later become the core of the collection of the Musée Picasso in Paris.

**25 Rue Victor Massé** (IX)    During the fall of 1900 Picasso enjoyed walking the streets of Paris. On one of these walks, only a short time after his arrival in the city, he met by chance the art dealer, Berthe Weill, who had her gallery at this address. She was a great champion of the modern artists and from this meeting Picasso was able to sell her three of his paintings of bullfights. She also introduced him to Pedro Mañach, a wealthy Catalan businessman who aspired to become an art dealer. He offered a small monthly contract for all Picasso's new paintings, which greatly pleased the penniless artist. Two years later Picasso exhibited here at Weill's gallery together with other artists, including Henri Matisse; unfortunately he did not sell anything at this time. Again in 1904 he was part of a group show here, exhibiting his drawing "Madman" which is today in the Picasso Museum in Barcelona. Today this building, with its sculpted façade, houses a nightclub.

**Moulin de la Galette, on Rue Lepic opposite Rue Tholozé** (XVIII)    In the 19th century this six-hundred-year-old windmill on the butte of Montmartre, once called Le Blute-Fin, was converted to a dancehall-restaurant which was mainly patronized by the working classes. Interestingly, two Catalan artists, Santiago Rusiñol and Ramon Casas, had lived in rooms above the dancehall in the early 1890s. During these years they divided their time between Paris and Barcelona, where they frequented the 4-Cats Café. Here they met with the young artists of that city, such as Picasso, and introduced them to the latest developments in the Paris art world. This influenced the development of the *modernista* style among the young Catalan artists. Picasso's first oil painting, done in Paris just before leaving to go home to Barcelona for the Christmas holidays in 1900, was a depiction of the dancers at the Moulin which is now in the Guggenheim Museum in New York. This work, one of his last in the *modernista* style, is very reminiscent of Henri Toulouse-Lautrec whom Picasso then greatly admired. Earlier paintings of the same locale were done by Auguste Renoir and Vincent van Gogh. Today the area is a private residential complex adorned with green garden trellises similar to those of the dancehall. The windmill can still be seen standing at the top of the hill. The arched wrought-iron gate bearing the name remains below on Rue Lepic and a nearby plaque tells the history of the mill.

**128 and 130 ter Boulevard de Clichy** (XVIII)    The building at #130 ter was the residence of Pedro Mañach, a Catalan businessman with whom Picasso had a contract. As a supplement to the small monthly salary, he allowed the artist and some of his friends to use studio space in this building. After Picasso and his friend Casagemas had spent the 1900 Christmas holiday in Barcelona, the latter returned to Paris earlier in 1901 than Picasso and settled in the studio here. Because his strong feelings for Germaine Gargallo were not mutual he became very despondent. On

*130 ter Boulevard de Clichy, an early Parisian residence
of Picasso*

February 17, at the café/restaurant L'Hippodrome, which was located nearby at **128 Boulevard de Clichy,** he shot himself in the presence of his beloved and two other Spanish friends. He died shortly afterward at the Hôpital Bichat-Claude-Bernard in Montmartre. When Picasso returned to Paris in spring, 1901, he moved in with Mañach at #130 ter. Here, stricken with grief over his friend's suicide, he began drawing pictures of the corpse he had not seen. A small oil painting of the death-bed scene is reminiscent of the style of Vincent van Gogh. Picasso now conceived his first unique style, the "blue period," which began with his painting "The

Burial of Casagemas;" this work is influenced by El Greco's masterpiece "The Burial of the Count Orgaz" with the satirical use of prostitutes in place of angels. Another early work in the blue style was "The Blue Room" which depicts the interior of Picasso's studio here; it is now in The Phillips Collection in Washington, D. C. In this same city at the National Gallery is a 1901 portrait of Mañach, who had become a father figure for the young artist.

**Hôpital St-Lazare, 107 bis Rue du Faubourg St-Denis** (X)    This hospital replaced the former 17th-century rectory which had been used as a prison since the time of the French Revolution and which was demolished in 1935. In the early 20th century it was a prison-hospital for women and many prostitutes were housed here, some with their infant children. In the fall of 1901 Picasso did many on-site studies of these women who fit the themes of isolation and abandonment depicted by his blue period. Some paintings based on these studies are: "Mother and Child," which hangs today in the Metropolitan Museum of Art in New York and is set next to the fountain that still stands in the hospital's courtyard; "Woman with a White Cap" which shows the hats which sufferers of venereal disease were compelled to wear; "Seated Woman and Child" which is now at the Fogg Museum at Harvard University; and "St-Lazare Woman by Moonlight" which now belongs to the Detroit Institute of Art.

✧**6 Rue Laffitte** (IX)    In 1901, thanks to the efforts of Pedro Mañach, Picasso had the good fortune to have his works shown here in the gallery of the art dealer Ambroise Vollard. The large exhibit presented seventy-five of his paintings, including many nudes. The young artist had produced many of these paintings in an intensely productive period of only three weeks. Despite the misgivings of Vollard, after having had a poorly-received Cézanne exhibit, the Picasso show was noticed by the critics. More than half of the works were sold and the presentation was favorably reviewed in *La Revue Blanche*, a liberal journal which was edited by Louis-Alfred Natanson. At this show Mañach introduced Picasso to the twenty-five-year-old poet, Max Jacob, who became his close friend despite the lack of a common language. In fact, Jacob is the person who taught Picasso to speak French. The building that housed the gallery is now gone.

**75 Rue des Martyrs** (XVIII)    This was the location of the popular night club, Divan Japonais, which Picasso visited in 1901. He did a painting of the dancers here in the style of Degas. This work was included in the Vollard show mentioned above. The site still houses the same type of establishment.

**Moulin Rouge, 82 Boulevard de Clichy** (XVIII)    This famous night spot, established in 1889, was visited by Picasso in 1901, at which time Josep

*Night view of Moulin Rouge, Paris*

Oller, a fellow-Catalan who was one of the club's managers, hired him to do a poster for the cabaret. Picasso himself preferred the simpler atmosphere of cabarets like Le Zut to the lavish surroundings he found at the Moulin Rouge.

**Place Jean-Baptiste Clément** (XVIII)   In the early 1900s the bar/restaurant Le Zut was located on the Rue Gabrielle side of this square; it was much frequented by Spanish artists. Behind the small gate, with the word "bière" in black, was a crude and dirty room with wobbly benches. The clientele tried to make it a bit more palatable by decorating the walls. Picasso's contribution was a drawing of a hermit surrounded by naked women which the group dubbed "The Temptation of St. Anthony." The likable owner, Frédé Gérard, would later open another night club, Lapin Agile (see below).

**Hôtel des Écoles, 3 Rue Champollion** (V)   In October, 1902, Picasso made his third attempt to succeed in Paris. When first arriving he stayed at this still-operating hotel on the Left Bank, far from the old haunts and friends of his earlier visits.

**57 Rue de Seine** (VI)   Picasso stayed only briefly at the Hôtel des Écoles in October, 1902. Because he had very little money he soon moved into the cheaper Hôtel du Maroc, which was located here. This hotel, also on the Left Bank, is now an apartment building.

**137 Boulevard Voltaire (XI)**   Picasso's 1902 journey to Paris was not successful; this was probably the lowest point of his career. His stark works of this time continue to reflect the sadness of the "blue period." To save money he soon moved in with his new friend, Max Jacob, who was living at this address over the shop where he worked. Because the apartment had only one large room with only one bed Picasso willingly worked all night while Jacob slept and slept during the day while Jacob was at his job.

**Boulevard Barbes, at corner of Place du Château Rouge (XVIII)**   While Picasso was living with Max Jacob in late 1902, the two moved here to a cheaper apartment. This building is located on a busy thoroughfare in Montmartre. In January, 1903, a broke and discouraged Picasso gave up and again returned home to Barcelona. After his return to Paris and a transition into his rose period in 1905, Jacob modeled for his bronze "Head of a Jester" which is now in the Philadelphia Museum of Art.

**Bateau-Lavoir, 13 Rue Ravignan (XVIII)**   In mid-1904 Picasso returned to Paris to stay. In his early days here he formed a relationship with a slender young woman named Madeleine who modeled for "Woman in a Chemise," "Seated Nude (Madeleine)" and "Woman Ironing." At this time he rented one of the myriad artists' studios in this former piano factory. From the rear the large rambling wooden building resembled the laundry boats

*Bateau-Lavoir, 13 Rue Ravignan, another early Paris residence*

on the Seine and thus was commonly called "Bateau-Lavoir." The building had no gas or electricity and a single water pump served all thirty-four tenants. It was at this pump that Picasso met his first long-term mistress, Fernande Olivier, with whom he lived for the next eight years. During the first five of these years the couple lived here in studio No. 7, sharing the tiny space with uncountable canvasses as well as two dogs and a pet mouse who was kept in a drawer. In 1904 their impoverished existence was poignantly depicted in his first etching, "The Frugal Meal," which can be seen in the Fine Arts Museum in Boston. In spite of these conditions the contented Picasso's work developed from the morose "blue period" through the more cheerful "rose period" and into the beginnings of cubism. In 1908 this studio was the site of a "banquet" in honor of painter Henri Rousseau, whose unique work Picasso admired. In 1970 the wooden structure burned down and the city rebuilt the complex in stone, now providing space for more prosperous artists. A building similar to the original Bateau-Lavoir may be seen around the corner at 1 Rue Orchampt. Photographs of the Bateau-Lavoir are on exhibit in the nearby **Montmartre Museum, 12 Rue Cortot.** Behind Bateau-Lavoir, at 6 Rue Garreau, one can enter a quiet courtyard with a view of the rear of the building. Across Place Émile-Goudeau from the studio was located the Café à l'Ami Émile where Picasso often ate with his poet friends Guillaume Apollinaire and Maurice Raynal.

**24 Rue Amsterdam** (VIII)    This was the location of the English Tavern which was a favorite gathering place of jockeys and others associated with horse racing. It was here that Picasso first met his close friend Guillaume Apollinaire in 1904. This poet and writer played a major role in introducing the cubist movement to the public.

**9 Rue Henner** (IX)    During the early 1900s Picasso was very friendly with the poet Guillaume Apollinaire and often attended parties at his home. One of his residences at this time was this attractive building on the corner of Rue Paul-Escudier with a café/bar on the ground floor. Another residence was at **37 Rue Gros** (XVI) but this has been replaced by a modern building.

**8 Rue Ravignan** (XVIII)    Around 1904, when this building housed the Restaurant Azon, Picasso frequently ate here. It was located just opposite the house where his good friend Max Jacob later lived at #7. Another favorite eating place at this time was Restaurant Vernin on Rue Cavallotti.

**Le Lapin Agile, 22 Rue des Saules** (XVIII)    During his time in Montmartre, Picasso often came to this former 18th-century coach inn. It was originally called the Cabaret des Assassins until 1880 when it was renamed for the creator of its colorful sign, André Gill. An early blue-period

*Le Lapin Agile, Montmartre cabaret, Paris*

Picasso work, entitled "The Woman with the Crow," is a portrait of Margot Marguerite Luc, the daughter of the owner, Frédé Gérard. This 1904 painting is now in the Toledo Museum of Art, in Ohio. A later work, which Picasso exchanged for some meals, was "Au Lapin Agile" which depicted both the painter and his host. After several changes in ownership, this work was sold at auction in 1989 for over $40 million! One morning, in the wee hours, the street outside the cabaret rang with gunshots when Picasso celebrated his first substantial sale by firing a pistol which he often carried. Visitors to Montmartre can still find entertainment at this cabaret.

**La Maison Rose, 2 Rue de l'Abreuvoir** (XVIII)    Another restaurant that Picasso often patronized during his Montmartre years was this lovely pink house with its outdoor tables on the corner of Rue des Saules. A history plaque outside the building describes its connection to artist Maurice Utrillo who, like Picasso, lived nearby.

✧ **63 Boulevard de Rochechouart** (IX)    During the years that he lived at the Bateau-Lavoir, Picasso became an ardent fan of the Cirque Medrano, the circus that once occupied this site. He attended as often as three times a week and did many paintings on this subject during his rose period. One of these works was a portrait of Clovis Sagot, a former clown who first bought this circus in 1897 and then later became an art dealer. In the square just down Rue des Martyrs from the circus was a small art shop owned by Père Soulie. Here Picasso sold some of his works and discovered his first Henri Rousseau painting in 1904.

✧**37 Boulevard Haussmann** (IX)   In 1905 Picasso exhibited some of his circus paintings here at Galerie Serrurier, including "The Family Saltimbanques." The harlequin clown in this work is a self-portrait of Picasso and the painting is now in the National Gallery in Washington, D.C. The site of the former gallery is now occupied by the large department store, Marks & Spencer.

✧**46 Rue Laffitte** (IX)   Here was located the art shop of Clovis Sagot, former clown and later owner of the Cirque Medrano. Around 1906 he sold Picasso's "Young Girl with a Basket of Flowers" to Gertrude and Leo Stein. Although the sister and brother argued about the quality of this work, Leo bought it despite Gertrude's objections. However, this would be the first of many Picasso paintings bought by the American writer who soon became a longtime friend of the artist.

**Closerie des Lilas, 171 Boulevard du Montparnasse** (VI)   Even before moving to this neighborhood from Montmartre, Picasso and his friends would sometimes spend an evening at this popular restaurant. Today many of the tables have small brass plates bearing the names of the many artists and writers who frequented this café that reached the peak of its popularity just before World War I.

**Jardin des Plantes** (V)   This lovely garden, which contains over 10,000 species of plants, was established by the doctors of Louis XIII in the 17th century. During the French Revolution the animals were moved from the Royal Court at Versailles to the English section of this garden. This zoo still remains one of the garden's principal attractions. Picasso, who was a great animal lover, found much inexpensive entertainment here during the lean years of his early career in Paris. He particularly liked the monkeys whom he considered to be caricatures of people. In 1905 he did a painting, "Harlequin's Family with an Ape," which was one of the early purchases of his work by Leo Stein and led to the longtime association between the artist and the Stein coterie.

**27 Rue de Fleurus** (VI)   It was here that the American expatriate writer Gertrude Stein lived, first with her brother Leo and later with her companion Alice Toklas. Her ground-floor flat, adjoining the garden, was a gathering place for many artists and writers. Picasso and Stein had a long and sometimes stormy friendship beginning in 1905. Shortly after their meeting she sat for a portrait by him. Despite the extraordinary number of sittings he eventually completed her face from memory. She hung this painting in a prominent place in her salon among the many works which she

*27 Rue de Fleurus, Paris apartment of Gertrude Stein*

bought from other artists such as Matisse, Renoir, Cézanne, Gauguin and Toulouse-Lautrec. The Picasso portrait is now in the Metropolitan Museum of Art, in New York City. It was at a gathering at this house in 1905 that Picasso first met Henri Matisse who became a lifelong friend. Picasso would later claim that Matisse was his only living rival. A plaque on the exterior of the building commemorates Stein's residence here.

**7 Rue Ravignan** (XVIII)   This was the home of poet Max Jacob from 1907 to 1911. During these years Picasso was a very close friend and visited him often. Today there is a plaque here noting Jacob's residence.

✧**2 Rue Lamarck** (XVIII)   This was the site of the Savoyarde Café, named for the bell of the nearby Basilique Sacré Coeur. Around 1907 it was a regular eating place of Picasso as well as the location of Max Jacob's regular Wednesday "parties."

**Musée d'Arts d'Afrique et d'Océanie, 293 Ave Daumesnil** (XII) Introduced to African art by Henri Matisse, Picasso's exposure to the works at the former Museum of Ethnology had an influence on his so called "Negro Period" of 1907. The collection was moved to its present site in the 1930s.

**9 Rue Constantinople** (VIII)   This lovely building, now a hotel, was often visited by Picasso when it was the 1908 residence of his friend, Guillaume

Apollinaire. At that time Picasso played matchmaker by introducing the poet to painter Marie Laurencin; the two became inseparable for the next five years. She painted a group portrait called "Group of Artists" which included herself and Apollinaire along with Picasso and his mistress, Fernande Olivier. This painting is now in the Baltimore Museum of Art.

✧**28 Rue Vignoy** (VIII)   The first cubist painting of Georges Braque was exhibited here in the small art shop of Daniel Henry Kahnweiler in 1907. During this exhibition Apollinaire took the artist to Bateau-Lavoir and introduced him to Picasso. This meeting was the start of a five-year close working relationship between the two men who would fully develop the style of cubism. Their unique creations were shown only at this gallery. It was here in 1909 that the public first saw Picasso's 1907 revolutionary painting "Les Demoiselles d'Avignon." The friendship of Kahnweiler and Picasso endured for sixty years.

**11 Boulevard de Clichy** (IX)   In 1908 Picasso sold more paintings to Gertrude Stein and the following year he had a successful exhibit in Munich. Based on these successes he and his mistress, Fernande Olivier, moved from Bateau-Lavoir to an apartment in this building. Here they had the luxury of a separate bedroom (rather than a curtained-off part of the studio) and were even able to afford a maid. Their entertaining here included visits by Henri Matisse and Gertrude Stein.

**7 Place du Calvaire** (XVIII)   The Italian restaurant, Au Coucou, was located in the left corner of this square which is adjacent to Place de Tertre on the Butte in Montmartre. Picasso and his friends had many lunches here during the years of 1910–1914. The building, now rundown, still has a lookout tower on the roof as it did then but access from the square has disappeared.

**101 Rue Caulaincourt** (XVIII)   Georges Braque had a studio here in the former Hôtel Roma in 1910, when he and Picasso were working almost inseparably at their new style, cubism. This name was coined by Henri Matisse when he was on the jury of the 1908 Salon d'Automne which rejected Braque's painting "Houses at L'Éstaque." During this period many unsigned paintings of Braque and Picasso were mistaken for the work of the other. The two cubists remained close friends although Picasso's work had largely moved away from cubism by 1920 when he entered his neo-classical period. Braque continued to work in the cubist style throughout his career. This nicely decorated turn-of-the-century red brick building at the corner of Rue Pierre-Dac is now the Hôtel Sacré Coeur. Braque later had another Montmartre studio at **5 Villa de Guelma (formerly Impasse de Guelma)**. He was at this impressive building in 1911–1912. In 1914, just before enlisting in the army, Braque moved to a third Montmartre location at **10 Rue Simon-Dereure (formerly Rue de l'Abreuvoir)**. This would be the last place that the two cubists would work with each other.

**Maison d'Arrêt de la Santé, 42 Rue de la Santé** (XIII)   In this prison, which is still in operation, Guillaume Apollinaire was held overnight when arrested for stealing some statues from the Louvre in late 1911; Picasso was his accomplice in this prank and was found in possession of one of the stolen items. After a prolonged investigation the charges against both men were eventually dropped.

✧ **6–8 Boulevard de Clichy** (XVIII)   The former Ermitage Café, located here, was one of Picasso's favorites. In 1912 he was here with Fernande Olivier, his mistress of eight years, and another couple when they impulsively decided to switch lovers. His new lover, Marcelle Humbert, whom he called Eva, remained his mistress until her untimely death of tuberculosis in 1915. Before disappearing, the café was for a while named Café Picasso.

**5 bis Rue Schoelcher** (XIV)   In 1912, after taking up with his new mistress, "Eva," Picasso moved with her to a studio apartment overlooking the Montparnasse Cemetery. Although far from Montmartre, this area of Paris was also home to many artists. This was Picasso's residence for four years; his lover died at the hospital in Auteuil in the winter of 1915.

**Café du Dôme, 108 Boulevard du Montparnasse** (XIV)   This elegant café opened in 1897 and hosted such luminaries as Lenin and Trotsky. Picasso and his friends began frequenting the café in 1912 when he moved to the Montparnasse area of the city. In later years, during the 1920s, it became the meeting place for many expatriate American artists and writers.

**Café Rotonde, 105 Boulevard du Montparnasse** (XIV)   This café was created from the owner's former shoe store when his stock of footwear was depleted in 1911. Just as the one above, it was patronized by Picasso after he moved to this part of the city. The square adjacent to both these establishments, where the Boulevard Raspail crosses Boulevard Montparnasse, is now named **Place Pablo Picasso**.

✧ **242 Boulevard Raspail** (XIV)   In 1913 Picasso took a studio here just around the corner from his Rue Schoelcher apartment. The building has since been replaced.

**278 Boulevard Raspail** (XIV)   Just down the boulevard from Picasso's new studio, this ornate 1903 building housed the office of *Soirées*, a magazine run by Serge Sérat and Baroness D'Oettingen. Picasso was among the many artists and writers who frequently visited here.

**Hôtel des Ventes Drouot, 9 Rue Drouot** (IX)   In 1914 some of Picasso's paintings were sold here at this French equivalent of Sotheby's. His position as an artist was elevated by the substantial prices commanded, especially that of his rose-period work "The Family Saltimbanques." The former hôtel has been replaced by a modern facility with the same function.

✧**61 Rue Notre-Dame-des-Champs** (VI)   This modern school, run by the nuns of Notre-Dame-de-Sion, occupies the former location of the convent of this order. On February 18, 1915, Picasso was godfather to Max Jacob, his Jewish poet friend, who converted to Catholicism at that time. The baptism was held in the chapel of this convent. Today the convent is located at #71 on the same street.

**174 Rue du Faubourg-St-Honoré** (VIII)   This was the location of the Galerie Barbazanges. In July, 1916, André Salmon organized here an exhibit called "L'Art Moderne en France," also known as the Salon D'Antin. This was the first major showing of Picasso's revolutionary masterpiece, "Les Demoiselles d'Avignon," which he had done in 1907.

**17 and 21 Rue de la Paix** (II)   These two locations were once fashion shops of Jacques Doucet, who was in this business from 1871 to 1929. The business had begun with the lace shop of his grandmother at #17 and later expanded to included clothes for women and men. This third-generation couturier was a lover and collector of impressionist and avant-garde art works and bought Picasso's landmark painting "Les Demoiselles d'Avignon," which he hung in a place of honor in his house in the suburb of Neuilly-sur-Seine. The Rue de la Paix is still a fashionable shopping area near the Opera House.

**Hôpital Militaire Val-de-Grâce, 74 Boulevard de Port-Royal** (V)   In 1916 poet Guillaume Apollinaire was wounded in action and confined in this large military hospital which is still in operation. Picasso visited his dear friend here and did a drawing of him with his head swathed in bandages called "Apollinaire Trepanned."

**198–200 Avenue de Maine** (XIV)   Picasso, Juan Gris, Max Jacob and others organized a banquet honoring Apollinaire on December 31, 1916. It was held here in an opulent café/restaurant, the Palais d'Orléans. The palace is now the social center of a major labor union.

✧**6 Rue Huyghens** (XIV)   This was the former location of the studio of Émile Lejeune where Picasso and other artists who were not in the army gathered frequently during World War I. The Lycée Paul Bert now occupies the site.

**Théâtre du Chatelet, 1 Place du Chatelet** (I)   In early 1917 Picasso designed the sets and curtain for *Parade*, a ballet by Jean Cocteau. Picasso attended the opening of the show here in May. During this project he met and fell in love with Olga Koklova, a dancer in the Ballets Russes. After following the ballet on its tour of Europe, he married her in 1918. This theater is still operating and is one of the city's most prominent.

**Mairie du VIe Arrondissement, 78 Rue Bonaparte** (VI)   This municipal building, built in the mid-19th century, was the site of the civil ceremony for Picasso's marriage to Russian ballerina Olga Koklova on July 12, 1918. The witnesses were Max Jacob, Jean Cocteau and Guillaume Apollinaire.

**Cathédrale Russe St-Alexandre-Newski, 12 Rue Daru** (VIII)   This 19th-century Byzantine-style cathedral was the venue for the religious cere-

*Russian Orthodox Cathedral in Paris*
*where Picasso was married in 1918*

*Café de Flore, Paris*

mony of the Picasso-Koklova wedding in July, 1918. Among those attending the elaborate celebration were Gertrude Stein and Alice Toklas, artists Henri Matisse and Georges Braque and Serge de Diaghilev, director of the Ballets Russes. Guillaume Apollinaire was Picasso's best man.

**Hôtel Lutétia, 43–45 Boulevard Raspail** (VI)   For a short time in 1918 Picasso and his new wife stayed here while waiting for their apartment on Rue La Boétie to be available. The opulent hotel is still operating but is now called the Lutétia-Concorde.

**23 Rue La Boétie** (VIII)   After their marriage the Picassos moved into a sixth-floor apartment in this building. The artist felt a bit constrained by the new middle-class environment and soon rented an additional studio in the eaves above the apartment to have a private place to work. The studio was locked to everyone. He had business contacts on both sides of his building: at #21 with gallery-owner Paul Rosenberg and at #25 with publisher Albert Skira. Although he lived here only until 1937, Picasso kept the studio for storage until 1951 when the postwar housing shortage led to his eviction.

**Café de Flore, 172 Boulevard St-Germain** (VI)   This still-operating café was the site of weekly meetings led by Picasso's friend Guillaume Apollinaire. These were attended every Tuesday afternoon by many writers and artists, including Picasso. In the 1930s, more than a decade after

Apollinaire's death, Picasso came to this café almost nightly, sitting at the second table in front of the main door.

**202 Boulevard St-Germain** (VII)    Picasso's close friend Apollinaire lived in this building from 1913 until his death on November 9, 1918. During these years the poet wrote numerous articles supporting cubism, the painting technique which Picasso and a few others were practicing at the time. The building today has a plaque in his remembrance.

**Église St-Thomas-d'Aquin, Place St-Thomas-d'Aquin** (VII)    In 1918, this large Renaissance-style church was the location of two events important to Picasso. In March he and art dealer Ambroise Vollard were witnesses at the wedding of Guillaume Apollinaire and Jacqueline Kolb. Eight months later the artist and his wife would attend Apollinaire's funeral here. The cortege proceeded through the streets of Paris which were decorated for the armistice celebration. The war in which the poet was severely wounded had ended two days after his death from influenza.

**Cimetière Père-Lachaise, 16 Rue du Repos** (XX)    At least three close associates of Picasso rest in this major Parisian cemetery. In November, 1918, he attended the funeral of his poet-friend Guillaume Apollinaire here. The other two were the Italian artist Amedeo Modigliani who died in 1920 and poet Paul Eluard who died in 1953.

**108 Rue La Boétie** (VIII)    This building, now occupied by France Telecom, was the location of Galerie Paul-Guillaume where Picasso and Henri Matisse had a joint exhibit of their work in 1918. Guillaume had had an earlier gallery at **16 Avenue de Villiers** in 1916. The collection of this dealer today forms the basis of the museum in the Orangerie on the Place de la Concorde and includes many paintings by Picasso.

**21 Rue La Boétie** (VIII)    In 1919 Picasso established a relationship with a new dealer, Paul Rosenberg, whose gallery was located in this attractive building next door to the artist's home. In the fall of that year the gallery presented a very successful Picasso exhibit. The works shown were in his new style, neoclassicism, marking the end of his cubist period. In 1939 an exhibit of twenty floral still-lifes by Picasso took place here.

**Hôpital Lariboisière, 2 Rue Ambroise-Paré** (X)    On January 27, 1920, Picasso's friend Max Jacob was taken to this hospital for treatment after being struck by an automobile. At the time of the accident he was on his way to the Opera to see Manuel de Falla's *Tricorne* for which Picasso had designed the sets.

**Opéra Garnier, Place de l'Opéra** (IX)    This magnificent opera house was the largest theater in the world at the time of its opening in 1875. In 1920 Picasso designed sets for two of its productions, De Falla's *Tricorne* and

Stravinsky's *Pulcinella*. While working on the latter he did a pencil sketch of the composer which is now at the Picasso Museum in Paris. It was now part of Picasso's lifestyle to attend grand events like opening nights and the parties associated with them.

**3–5 Rue Papin** (III)   Another production for which Picasso did the designs was the ballet *Cuadro Flamenco*, which opened here at the former Théâtre Gaîté-Lyrique in the fall of 1920. This historic theater, built on Square Émile-Chautemps in 1861–1862, closed in 1958 but now has reopened as a children's theater called La Planète Magique. The exterior of the building has been restored and bears a commemorative plaque.

**13 Avenue Montaigne** (VIII)   In 1920 Picasso participated in an exhibition of dada works at the Galerie Montaigne which was located in the same building as the Théâtre Champs-Elysées.

✧**29 bis Rue d'Astory** (VIII)   During the years of cubism Daniel Henry Kahnweiler was the primary purveyor of these paintings. Later, in 1920, still Picasso's close friend and dealer, he opened his Galerie Simon at this new address. During the German occupation it was renamed Galerie Louise-Leiris, using the name of Kahnweiler's sister-in-law to avoid the restrictions on Jewish-owned businesses.

**Théâtre de l'Atelier, 1 Place Charles-Dullin** (XVIII)   This theater hosted the premiere of Jean Cocteau's modern adaptation of *Antigone* in the winter of 1922. Picasso, who was a close friend of Cocteau, did the set decoration for the production. This historic theater, founded by actor-director Charles Dullin, is still in operation.

**10 Rue d'Anjou** (VIII)   This building, now housing offices, was the home of Jean Cocteau around 1922 at the time of the production of *Antigone*. He and Picasso, who met in 1916, were friends for over forty years.

**28 Rue Boissy d'Anglas** (VIII)   Picasso and his wife, along with many of their friends, attended the gala opening of Le Boeuf sur le Toit which moved to this location in 1922. It was a very popular night spot during the 1920s. This dada-inspired club, co-owned by Jean Cocteau, was named for his circus ballet. It was first located nearby at **34 Rue du Colisée**.

**29 Rue du Faubourg-St-Honoré** (VIII)   After 1925 Coco Chanel, successful fashion designer, lived on the ground floor of this former mansion. The entrance, inside the courtyard, is adorned with an ornate glass canopy. In her sumptuous apartment Chanel always kept a room available for her friend Picasso's use. The two had worked together on Jean Cocteau's *Antigone* in 1922, he designing the sets and she the costumes for the production.

**23 Rue des Grands-Augustins** (VI)   This apartment building with its old romanesque-style portal was one of the Paris homes of American landscape architect Gerald Murphy and his socialite wife, Sara. They were said to be the models for F. Scott Fitzgerald's Dick and Nicole Diver in his novel *Tender Is the Night.* Picasso had met this wealthy pair in 1921; during the summer of 1923, they were living at the opulent Hôtel du Cap in Antibes where the Picassos were also staying. Picasso was allegedly infatuated with Sara Murphy and she may have inspired many of his works during the early 1920s, particularly the large female nudes. Gerald Murphy, then aspiring to be a painter, was intrigued by the modernistic art of Picasso but he himself painted in the precisionist style of pop art for some nine years before giving up his painting for the business world.

❖ **42 Rue Fontaine** (IX)    This was formerly the site of the 1920s residence of André Breton, leader of the dada and surrealist movements. Although Picasso involved himself to some degree in both of these, he never fully embraced either one. Breton's 4th-floor apartment was decorated with paintings by Picasso, Braque, Seurat and Chirico. The present building dates from 1930.

**40 ter Rue Fabert** (VII)    From 1927 to 1939 this building, then the Hôtel de la Gare des Invalides, housed the editorial offices of *Transition.* This avant-garde literary journal was produced by Eugène Jolas and Elliot Paul, editors of the *Paris Tribune.* Illustrations for the magazine were done by such artists as Picasso, Joan Miró, Henri Matisse, Piet Mondrian, Alexander Calder and Hans Arp.

**44 Rue Jacob** (VI)    During the 1920s Picasso also did art work for the international journal *Little Review.* It was founded and run by Margaret Anderson who was fined for publishing obscene matter in 1920 when the journal printed some excerpts from James Joyce's *Ulysses.* Her Paris office was located here in what was then the Hôtel Jacob; today it is the Hôtel Angleterre.

**Théâtre Michel, 38 Rue des Mathurins** (VIII)    This theater was the location of the 1920s meetings of the dada art movement. Although he never became an exponent of this style, Picasso did attend some of these gatherings.

**36 Rue Bonaparte** (VI)    In 1924 Picasso's close friend Jean Cocteau lived in Room 6 of this establishment. It was then called the Hôtel Napoléon Bonaparte, not to be confused with newer Hôtel Napoléon located nearby. Today it is called the Hôtel St-Germain-des-Prés.

**Librairie Gallimard, 15 Boulevard Raspail** (VII)    In 1924 the owner of this still-operating bookstore published *La Revolution Surrealiste* at this site. Artists contributing illustrations included Picasso and Max Ernst.

**Théâtre Champs-Elysées, 15 Avenue Montaigne** (VIII)    This theater, which opened in 1918, served for a time as the city's main concert hall and hosted the Ballets Russes performances. It was frequently attended by Picasso and his wife during the 1920s. In 1924 an enlargement of Picasso's painting "The Race" was used as the front curtain for the ballet, *The Blue Train*, and he did the illustrations for the program. The costumes for this production were designed by his friend Coco Chanel.

**13 Rue Bonaparte** (VI)    This was the original location of Galerie Pierre, founded by Pierre Loeb. Picasso participated in the first surrealist exhibition held here in November, 1925. The show created such a heated reaction that police were required to restore order outside the gallery. Today there is another gallery here.

**2 Rue des Beaux-Arts (14 Rue de Seine)** (VI)    The Galerie Pierre moved to this address in 1926 and remained in business here until 1964. During the late 1920s and the 1930s Picasso was represented in several group exhibitions here. He had individual shows here in 1927, 1937 and 1939. Another gallery now occupies the premises.

**16 Rue Jacques-Callot** (VI)    This was the location of the Surrealiste Galerie where Picasso participated in an exhibit in 1926 with fellow Spaniard Joan Miró and others.

**44 Rue La Boétie** (VIII)    In the early 1930s Picasso maintained an apartment in this building for his new mistress, Marie-Thérèse Walter, the daughter of a Swedish diplomat whom he had first met on the sidewalk outside Galeries Lafayette department store in 1927. At the time he lived just down the street with his wife, Olga. In 1935 his mistress bore him a daughter, Maya, and he divorced his wife. Although he wished to marry Marie-Thérèse he did not because he feared that the resulting excommunication would deprive him of his Spanish citizenship. Not long after his divorce he began his affair with Dora Maar.

❖ **8 Rue de Sèze** (IX)    This building, once having its entrance at 12 Rue Godot de Mauray, was the site of the prestigious Galerie Georges-Petit. It was here in 1932 that Picasso had his first retrospective exhibit. This successful event was the first opportunity for the Parisian public to see the entire spectrum of works by this artist. The show included over two hundred paintings and was also later presented in Zurich. The building has since been modernized and substantially changed.

**25 Rue La Boétie** (VIII)    In June, 1933, this was the office of the new journal, *Minotaure*. Picasso did a cover design for the maiden issue which was entirely devoted to him. The journal was published and edited by Albert Skira. The symbol of the minotaur, a mythical creature half bull and half man, was widely employed around this time to denote the bestial-

*Café des Deux Magots, Paris*

ity of the human race. In 1935 Picasso did a masterful series of etchings using this theme which today can be seen in the Picasso Museum in Paris.

**Café des Deux Magots, 170 Boulevard St-Germain** (VI)   This popular café has been operating at this location since 1873. In the mid-1930s it was a favorite meeting-place for surrealist artists. Picasso, who sometimes attended these gatherings, met his mistress Dora Maar here in 1936. A plaque outside the café explains its history.

**Brasserie Lipp, 151 Boulevard St-Germain** (VI)   This charming tavern with its smartly decorated interior was established here in 1880. During the Spanish Civil War, in the late 1930s, Picasso met here occasionally with Russian painter Marc Chagall. He also had a farewell lunch here in 1939 before moving to Royan to avoid the German invasion of World War II. A plaque describing the restaurant's history can be found outside the building.

**17 Quai Voltaire** (VII)   American composer Virgil Thomson lived in the attic of this narrow building from 1927 to 1940. During this time he hosted popular Friday afternoon parties which were attended by many artsy personalities including Picasso. Thomson composed the musical score for *Four Saints in Three Acts*, an opera written by Picasso's friend and admirer Gertrude Stein.

**Hôtel d'Hercule, 7 Rue des Grands-Augustins** (VI)    In 1937 Picasso rented a studio apartment in this 17th-century mansion. Recently divorced, he set up his latest mistress, Dora Maar, in a nearby apartment. While living here he painted his masterpiece "Guernica," a moving artistic condemnation of the brutal bombing of that Spanish city by Nazi planes. Picasso had been familiar with this town in which over two thousand civilians were killed by the attack. The painting was exhibited in the Spanish pavilion of the 1937 World Fair. The entire period of his work on this immense canvas was recorded photographically by Ms. Maar. Later, during the German occupation of Paris, a German official visited Picasso's studio here. Seeing

*Picasso's residence at 7 Rue des Grands-Augustins, Paris*

the painting he asked the artist if he had done this; Picasso replied, "No, you did." Despite the later efforts of Cultural Minister André Malraux to preserve the studio as a monument to Picasso, the building is now used as government offices. Outside is a plaque denoting the artist's residence here from 1937 to 1954.

**6 Rue de Savoie** (VI)   This was the location of the apartment of Dora Maar, Picasso's mistress from 1936 to 1946. She was the most well-educated of all his lovers, having studied art and photography at the finest schools in Paris. She also was fluent in both French and Spanish.

**Jardins du Trocadero, Avenue des Nations-Unies** (XVI)   These gardens in front of the newly built Palais de Chaillot were the site of the Spanish pavilion at the 1937 World Fair. At this event, in the middle of the Spanish Civil War, Picasso's masterpiece "Guernica" had its first public showing under the auspices of the besieged Spanish republic.

**31 Rue de Seine** (VI)   Picasso participated in the grand opening of Galerie Gradiva at this location in 1937. The exhibit was organized by André Breton and included fellow Spaniard Salvador Dalí.

**11 Rue Foyatier** (XVIII)   During 1939 Picasso came here regularly to the Atelier Lacourière to work on the illustrations for a book of his writings. He later had the necessary equipment moved to his studio on Grands-Augustins. The printing workshop, located along a stairway on the butte of Montmartre, is still in operation.

**5 Rue Christine** (VI)   Gertrude Stein and Alice Toklas moved into this 17th-century building in 1938 when they were evicted from their Rue de Fleurus flat. Stein's extensive collection of modern art came with them but was left behind in the apartment when the women fled to the South of France during the war. Shortly before liberation in 1944 a group of Gestapo raided the premises looking for its occupants. When all they found were her paintings they denounced the Picassos as "Jewish trash, good for burning." Among these was his cubist painting "The Guitar on the Table," which is now in the Hood Museum at Dartmouth College. The women returned to this apartment after liberation; Stein died in 1946 but Toklas remained here until 1964.

**16 Boulevard des Italiens** (II)   During World War II this building was the location of the Banque du Commerce et de l'Industrie. Picasso and Henri Matisse stored their paintings in the bank's vault to protect them from the German occupiers.

**16 Rue des Grands-Augustins** (VI)   During the war Picasso opened a black-market restaurant, Le Catalan, in this small building near his residence and he and Dora ate there every night. It was here in 1943 that he met 21-year-old Françoise Gilot, who would soon become his next mistress.

**Boulevard Henri IV** (IV)  In an apartment here, at the tip of Ile St-Louis, Picasso maintained his former mistress, Marie-Thérèse Walter, and their daughter, Maya. He visited them here weekly and in 1938 did a portrait of the child with a doll.

**Église St-Roch, 296 Rue St-Honoré** (I)  In 1944 Picasso attended memorial services in this 17th-century church for Max Jacob who died in a German prison camp. Some mutual acquaintances are said to have resented the fact that Picasso, despite having some influential German friends, had not tried to have Jacob released. Others, however, thought him courageous to risk possible reprisal by the Germans for attending this service.

**Chez Francis, 7 Place de l'Alma** (VIII)  In 1946 Picasso took Dora Maar and his new love, Françoise Gilot, to this riverside establishment for a luncheon. After a public scene between the women, Picasso ended his waning affair with Dora. The reassured Françoise moved into his Grands-Augustins studio shortly thereafter. The still-operating seafood restaurant was completely renovated in the 1980s but the great view of the Eiffel Tower from the terrace remains the same.

**2 Rue de l'Élysée** (VIII)  This large decorated building is an annex to the Élysée Palace, the nation's presidential residence since 1873. In November, 1948, there was an exhibition here of 150 pieces of Picasso's ceramics done at Vallauris. The exhibition was sponsored by the Maison de la Pensée Française.

**Galerie Louise-Leiris, 47 Rue de Monceau** (VIII)  After World War II this gallery, still run by Daniel Kahnweiler and his sister-in-law, moved here. In 1949 Kahnweiler made a contract with Françoise Gilot to sell her paintings. Picasso resented this action by his old associate since it gave his mistress more independence than he wanted her to have. Although the building has been replaced by a modern one the gallery is still operating there under the same name. Exhibits of Picasso's works in the gallery's collection are occasionally held.

**Salle Pleyel, 252 Rue du Faubourg-St-Honoré** (VIII)  This major concert hall was the venue for the World Peace Congress in 1949. The Congress was sponsored by the Communist Party which Picasso had joined in 1945 because of its active role against the German occupation during the war. In 1949, in honor of his newborn daughter, Paloma (Spanish for pigeon), the artist had done a painting of this bird. When the organizer of the Congress came to Picasso's studio to discuss his creating a symbol for the occasion he immediately chose this painting which was then entitled "Dove." It was used on all literature and advertising for the Congress. Picasso attended these annual meetings from 1948 to 1951, involving trips to Poland, England and Italy.

**9 Rue Gay-Lussac** (V)   Picasso acquired an apartment in this building in 1950. His part-time residence here with Françoise Gilot dated from that year to 1954 and is commemorated by a plaque on the façade. He continued to use this flat on his trips to Paris from his post-war home in the South of France until 1967.

**École Alsacienne, 109 Rue Notre-Dame des Champs & 128 Rue d'Assas** (VI)   After Picasso's breakup with Françoise Gilot, she and their two children lived in Paris. During the 1950s the children attended this still-operating school.

**Maison de l'UNESCO, Place de Fontenoy** (VII)   This headquarters of the United Nations Educational, Scientific and Cultural Organization was built under the cooperation of many architects and artists from 1955 through 1958. The trapezoidal hall in the conference building is decorated with Picasso's mural "Victory of Light and Peace over Darkness and Death" (or "The Fall of Icarus"). The artist, who was seventy-six at the time, was at first reluctant to accept such a large commission but he eventually took on the project. The public areas of the building are open to visitors.

**Square Laurent-Prache** (VI)   This small garden, adjacent to the historic 11th-century church of St-Germain-des-Prés, has a sculpture by Picasso, "Head of a Woman." The monument has stood here since 1959 when it was donated to the city by the artist in memory of his friend Guillaume Apollinaire. He had done an earlier monument to the poet during the 1920s which was rejected. The wire construction of this project is today in the Picasso Museum in Paris.

**Galerie Berggrüen, 70 Rue de l'Université** (VII)   In 1964 this was the site of an exhibit "Sixty Years of Engravings by Picasso." The gallery is still in operation today.

**Petit Palais, Avenue Winston-Churchill** (VIII)   In 1966 a Picasso retrospective exhibit in honor of his eighty-fifth birthday was held at the Grand Palais. Because of the great number of works included, the sculptures were displayed at this nearby palace.

**Bibliothèque Nationale, 58 Rue de Richelieu** (II)   In 1868 the Hôtel Mazurin was restored and enlarged by architect Henri Labrouste to accommodate the National Library of France which owns over twelve million volumes. The most impressive addition at that time was the beautiful reading room designed of iron and glass. In 1966, in coordination with the Picasso retrospective at the Grand Palais, this historic library mounted an exhibition of Picasso's etchings, engravings, etc.

*Picasso's monument to Apollinaire in Square Laurent-Prache, Paris*

**Musée Carnavalet, 23 Rue de Sévigné** (III)    This 17th-century mansion houses an extensive collection depicting the history of the city of Paris from prehistoric times to the present. Among the myriad items seen here is Picasso's painting "Le Vert Galant" (1943), which looks from the park at the western tip of Ile de la Cité up to the equestrian statue of Henri IV in Place du Pont-Neuf.

**Musée Maillol, 59–61 Rue de Grenelle** (VII)    In addition to his own sculptures, this museum also exhibits items personally collected by Aristide Maillol. Among these are the following Picasso drawings: a still-life, a standing nude, hand (1920), apples and a small portrait of Honoré de Balzac.

★ **Musée National d'Art Moderne, Place Beaubourg** (IV)    This museum is housed in the controversial modernistic structure of the Georges Pompidou National Center of Art and Culture which opened in 1977. The collection spans the art movements of the 20th century from fauvism and cubism to the present day. The Picasso works here represent every decade of his career to 1956. The paintings include his striking 1901 portrait of Gustave Coquiot, a fashionable art and theater columnist. He wrote the introduction to the catalog for Picasso's first Paris exhibition at the Vollard gallery and was later responsible for designating Picasso's style into periods such as the "blue period" and the "rose period." In addition to the large number of paintings here, the museum also owns some drawings, collages and Picasso's theater curtain designed for Jean Cocteau's ballet, *Parade*, in 1917.

★ **Musée National de l'Orangerie, Place de la Concorde** (I)    This small museum houses the outstanding collection amassed by the art dealer Paul Guillaume, his widow and her second husband. Included are some one dozen paintings by Picasso. His blue period is represented by "The Embrace" (1903), his rose period by "The Adolescents" (1906) and his classical period by "The Great Bather" (1921). Of interest also is the striking 1915 portrait of Guillaume by Amedeo Modigliani, another friend of Picasso.

★ **Musée Picasso, 5 Rue de Thorigny** (III)    This museum, which opened in 1985, is located in the 17th-century Hôtel Salé in the city's historic Marais district. The collection is mainly works acquired by the State after the artist's death as payment of estate taxes. It consists of over two hundred paintings, more than three thousand drawings, eighty-eight ceramics and fifty-eight sculptures. Because these works had been kept by Picasso until his death, it can be assumed that many of them were especially important to him. Among these are portraits of many people who were close to him during his lifetime including his parents, wives, children, mistresses and friends which are exhibited on a rotated basis. There are also self-portraits here from 1901 and 1906 as well as paintings and drawings from all the periods of his life. His *Minotauromachie* series of etchings from 1935 is on display with related works. An entire room is devoted to his colorful ceramics, a medium which was important for him after World War II. Among the many sculptures here are a bronze bust of his first mistress, Fernande Olivier, done in 1906 and a series of masks sculpted in African style around 1907. In addition to the art works are many special items which include personal effects such as his chair, brushes and paint bowl, his letters to and from his friend Guillaume Apollinaire dating from 1905–1918 and many photos taken during his long life. There is also a rotating exhibit of the many works by other artists which were in his personal collection at the time of his death. Visitors to the museum can here view films on Picasso's life and work.

**Palais de Tokyo, 11 Avenue du Président Wilson** (XVI)   This palace, built in 1937, now houses the Museum of Modern Art of the City of Paris. The collection illustrates all the major trends in modern art. The style of cubism is represented by works of Braque as well as Picasso's "The Pigeon with the Peas" (1911) and "Head of a Man" (1912). In 1952 Picasso exhibited his "Goat" sculpture here as part of the Salon de Mai, which was originally established in 1945 at the Galerie Maurs, **3 Avenue Matignon.**

**Carrefour de la Croix-Rouge** (VI)   This square is the location of the monumental 1985 bronze sculpture by César entitled "Le Centaure, Homage to Pablo Picasso."

## Neuilly-sur-Seine

Neuilly-sur-Seine is a pleasant suburb which lies just west of Paris and north of the Bois de Boulogne. On its west it is bordered by the Seine which makes a horseshoe bend to the north after leaving the center of Paris. The town is quite accessible by a pleasant walk or by Metro Lines #1 or #3. At 33 Rue St-James was located the home of Jacques Doucet, who was in the fashion business from 1871 to 1929. A lover and collector of impressionist and avant-garde art works, he bought Picasso's landmark painting "Les Demoiselles d'Avignon" and hung it in a place of honor at the head of a crystal staircase in a specially built wing of this house. Unfortunately the mansion has been replaced by a modern apartment building; the painting is now in the Museum of Modern Art in New York. In 1965 Picasso spent his last stay in Paris at Neuilly in the **Hôpital Américain, 63 Boulevard**

**Victor-Hugo.** The octogenarian artist received treatment for a prostate disorder at this historic hospital in which many American expatriates have been treated.

## Boulogne-Billancourt

The suburb of Boulogne-Billancourt is located just west of Paris and south of the Bois de Boulogne. It is easily reached on foot or by Metro Line #10. Picasso's two children by Françoise Gilot were born here at the still-operating **Belvedere Clinic, 18 Rue Belvedere**. Claude was born in May, 1947, and Paloma in April, 1949.

*Belvedere Clinic, Boulogne-Billancourt, where two of
Picasso's children were born*

## St-Denis

The suburb of St-Denis lies to the north of the city and is accessible via Metro Line #13. The building of the Basilica of St-Denis was begun in 1140 on the site of former churches which existed there since 475 A.D. In addition to being an outstanding example of early gothic architecture the basilica houses the tombs of almost all of the French kings and queens and their families and is well worth a visit. The city's **Musée d'Art et d'Histoire, 22 bis Rue Gabriel-Péri,** is splendidly housed in a 17th-century former Carmellite convent. The exhibitions include a room dedicated to the poet, Paul Eluard, who was born in St-Denis in 1895. Since Picasso was a close friend of his, there are many items in the exhibit which relate to the artist. Among these are: a 1936 portrait drawn by Picasso of Eluard's second wife, Nasch; a book illustrated by Picasso and dedicated to the poet; a collection of surrealistic postcards, one of which was done by Picasso; a small 1936 abstract drawing of a woman which Picasso did for the magazine *Solidarite* for the benefit of the victims of the Spanish Civil War; a portrait of the poet by Françoise Gilot done in 1951; and a large ceramic vase with a minotaur design which was given by Picasso to his friend as a wedding gift in 1951 when he married his third wife, Dominique. The ongoing development of the museum promises to include an exhibit of modern art including at least one work by Picasso.

# CHAPTER SIX

# *The Eastern Pyrenees*

THE PYRENEES are high mountains that run two hundred seventy miles from the Atlantic Coast to the Mediterranean Coast along the Spanish-French border. In the eastern part of the range, north of the Spanish border, is an area that was part of the Kingdom of Catalonia until it was divided between France and Spain in 1659 by the Treaty of the Pyrenees. Today the spirit of Catalan nationalism is still very much alive in this region of France, just as it is in the Spanish region of Catalonia. Because of the geographic and cultural similarities between this part of France and the Catalan region of Spain, Picasso often spent holidays in the towns of the Eastern Pyrenees.

## *Céret*

Céret is a charming town at the foot of the Pyrenees very near the Spanish border. During the early 20th century Picasso was among the modern artists, many Catalan, who were drawn to this town by the presence of the sculptor Manuel Martínez Hugué (called Manolo) who had come here from his native Barcelona. Both men found the cultural aspects and the bullfights of Céret reminiscent of the Catalan capital. Picasso spent the summer of 1911 here with Fernande Olivier, his first long-term mistress, whom he had been with since 1904. By 1912 he had begun an affair with Marcelle Humbert (Eva) and she was his companion here during the summers of 1912 and 1913. During the latter stay Picasso heard of the death of his father in Barcelona, less than one hundred miles away, but chose not to attend his funeral. During his sojourns in Céret he continued to develop his cubist style in association with many other artists, including Georges Braque with whom he also worked in Paris. In later life, after settling in the South of France, Picasso occasionally visited Céret where he again attended bullfights.

### SPECIFIC SITES IN CÉRET

**72 Rue St-Ferréol.**   This building was once the Hotel du Canigou, a family pension owned by Armand Janer. In the summer of 1911, on his first visit to Céret, Picasso lived here for a month with his mistress Fernande Olivier.

**Maison Alcouffe, Avenue Francesc-Irla.**   In 1911, when Picasso first stayed in Céret, this house was the home of Frank Burty Haviland, a wealthy painter whose family originated in America. It is quite near the lovely Pont du Diable. Picasso often visited here with his friend Manolo and other artists.

**Maison Delcros, 3 Rue des Evadés de France.**   This large house, with extensive gardens, was rented by Frank Burty Haviland from 1912 to 1914. During the summers of 1912 and 1913 Picasso was among the artists that rented studios here. Because of its importance to that artistic style, the house was nicknamed the "House of the Cubists." The building still stands today in the high part of the town near Place des Tilleuls.

**Le Grand Café, Boulevard Maréchal Joffre at the corner of Rue St-Ferréol.**   This still-operating café was frequented by Picasso and the other artists of Céret. Here in the evenings they met and discussed the new works that

*"House of the Cubists" at 3 Rue des Evadés de France, Céret*

they were so diligently working on all day at their studios. Today the menu includes an ice cream specialty called "Coupe Picasso."

**Les Arènes, Rue des Arènes.**   This arena was the site of bullfights that Picasso attended during his summers in Céret. It is still in use for the same purpose. Near the stadium are two interesting statues. Across the street at the corner of Rue de la Sardane is the monument by Félip Vilà commemorating Picasso's "Dance of Peace," with the depiction of the Catalan folk-dance, the Sardana. At the other end of the bullring, in the Place de la Résistance, is a reproduction of Manolo's "Torero," of which the original is in the Céret Museum of Modern Art. In 1904, while both were in Paris, Picasso had done an ink drawing of this sculptor who was also from Catalonia.

*Monument to Picasso near the Céret bullring*

*Le Pont du Diable, Céret*

**Le Pont du Diable.** This impressive 14th-century bridge over the River Tech was seen and sketched by Picasso during his time in Céret.

**Le Pablo, 1 Place Picasso.** This bar, on the square named for Picasso, has a great number of modern art works adorning its walls. Among them is a Picasso sketch of a bullfight done in 1957.

★**Musée d'Art Moderne Céret, 8 Boulevard Maréchal Joffre.** This museum was founded in 1950 by artist Pierre Brune. The collection has been enriched by numerous donations from artists who spent time working in Céret, particularly Picasso and Matisse. The former donated fifty-three of his works to the museum. Among these is a series of twenty-eight small ceramic bowls depicting bullfighting with various effects of the sun; these were done at Vallauris in 1953. There is also a set of eight large terra cotta plates with similar scenes. In addition, there are many other ceramic pieces of various types including one with a white-on-white portrait of his wife, Jacqueline, done in 1956. Two oil paintings here are "Still-life with Skull and Pitcher" (1946) and "Portrait of Corina Pere Romeu" (1902). The collection also includes a terra cotta head of Picasso done by the Catalan sculptor Pablo Gargallo in 1913. In the entrance foyer of the museum is a chronology board (with English translation) describing the artists' connection to Céret and a case of memorabilia of these artists. There are also a number of large photos including one of Picasso attending a Céret bullfight in 1953.

*Hotel Les Templiers, Collioure*

## Collioure

In the early 1950s, while still at Vallauris, Picasso often traveled to the Mediterranean coast near the Spanish border. One of the towns he visited here was Collioure, a lovely seaside village where the fauvists, led by Henri Matisse and André Derain, had flourished some fifty years before. On one of these trips, in 1953, he was trying to escape from the tension of his breakup with Françoise Gilot. At that time he stayed at the celebrated

**Hôtel Les Templiers,** at 12 Quay de l'Amirante, just opposite the 12th-century castle of the Knights of the Templars. He swam daily at the nearby beach and hung out at the Café des Sports, which was owned by René Pou and located on Rue Colbert just behind the hotel. He also attended his favorite sporting event, the bullfights, in the **Arena** on Avenue Aristide Maillol near the railroad station.

## *Perpignan*

This old city is the capital of French Catalonia. Its proximity to the Spanish border and its history as the former residence of the Kings of Majorca have endowed it with an atmosphere as much Spanish as it is French. The Kings' immense 13th–14th-century palace, standing within a 16th-century citadel, is an impressive memorial to the Catalan rulers whose reign here ended only in 1659 and who still command much loyalty from the local population. Picasso, who had adopted Catalonia as his homeland, lived here for several summers during the 1950s.

### SPECIFIC SITES IN PERPIGNAN

**Musée Rigaud, 16 Rue de l'Ange.**   This museum is housed in the 17th-century former Hôtel Blanes which was the home of Count and Countess Jacques de Lazerme during the 1950s. Picasso, who had been introduced to this couple by fellow artist Pierre Brune, visited here during the summers of 1954–1956. While here, a large room overlooking the courtyard was put at his disposal to be used as a studio. During this time he did three drawings of his hostess dressed in Catalan costume which were given to the Count and Countess in gratitude for their hospitality. In 1979 the residence was converted into the city's art museum and the three drawings became part of the collection. Outside the museum is a plaque which relates the history of the building, including Picasso's connection to it.

**Gare SNCF, end of Avenue du Général de Gaulle.**   During the summer of 1954 Picasso and his long-time mistress Françoise Gilot had a final parting here when she took their two children and left for Paris. There is a history plaque here telling of fellow Spaniard Salvador Dalí's theory that the square in front of this station was the center of the Universe!

*Rigaud Museum, Perpignan, where Picasso lived and worked in the 1950s*

# CHAPTER SEVEN

# *Provence and the Mediterranean Coast*

THE SOUTH OF FRANCE, commonly referred to as the Midi, has long been a popular holiday region for most of the population. In addition to its mild climate, the area is rich in vestiges of the ancient settlements of the Greeks and Romans who founded many of the region's cities. Modern resort facilities exist side-by-side with medieval perched villages and Roman ruins. The Provence region is also noted for its delectable cuisine which features the use of local olive oil and garlic. Picasso found great inspiration in the ambience of the Mediterranean and was among the many who summered in the area as soon as he was able to afford it, from the 1920s onward. After World War II the Midi became his primary area of residence.

## *Avignon*

Avignon, known as the city of the Popes, is one of the most beautiful and artistic cities in all of France. It is famous for its 12th-century bridge which was the first to cross the Rhone in that vicinity; today only four of the bridge's twenty-two arches still stand. Picasso came here briefly in the summer of 1912 with his new mistress, Marcelle Humbert (called Eva), but they settled in nearby Sorgues. The couple returned to spend the summer of 1914 here with fellow artists Georges Braque and André Derain. World War I began that August and when his friends left to enlist in the army Picasso saw them off at the train station but did not join them in their venture. After the war the close working relationship between Picasso and Braque was never renewed. In 1970, near the end of Picasso's life, and again posthumously in 1975, exhibitions of his work were held here in the monumental Papal Palace.

*Papal Palace, Avignon, site of major Picasso exhibitions*

### SPECIFIC SITES IN AVIGNON

✧ **14 Rue St. Bernard.** This was the location of the building where Picasso lived with his mistress, Eva, in the summer of 1914. The city university has now expanded to encompass the site.

**Palais des Papes, Place du Palais.** This 14th-century palace is comprised of two large fortresses and covers 2.6 acres of ground. It is the major monument in the city which was the home of nine popes during the years 1309–1403. Picasso had often dreamed of having his work exhibited here and in 1970 the dream was realized. One hundred fifty paintings, many of which were recently done, were hung in the Clement VI Chapel of the palace. This was Picasso's last major exhibition before his death in 1973. A second Picasso exhibition, held posthumously, opened here in late 1975. During this show, on January 31, 1976, one hundred eighteen paintings were stolen from the palace but all were subsequently recovered. Today this Great Chapel, which may be visited as part of the tour of the palace, is still used for special exhibits.

**Hotel Mercure, Rocade Charles de Gaulle.** This hotel, located two kilometers south of the city on RN-7, was in August, 1976, a Holiday Inn. At that time it was the site of negotiations between the police and the art thieves who had stolen over one hundred Picasso paintings from the Papal Palace the previous January. These negotiations were probably due to the fact that the works were unsigned and difficult for the thieves to sell;

Picasso had the habit of not signing a work until it was sold and these late works had not been sold before his death. An agreement was reached to exchange the paintings for $2 million at a location in Marseille in October, 1976. During the transfer, the police succeeded in retrieving the paintings and capturing the thieves as well.

## Sorgues

This small town is located about ten kilometers north of Avignon. In the summer of 1912, not wholly comfortable in Céret due to social difficulties caused by his change of mistresses, Picasso came to Avignon with Eva. A tram, which ran between the city and this nearby town, was called the "Buffalo" because of its American West styling. Picasso was charmed by its open-air cars which were similar to the *Jardineres* used in Barcelona. To optimize their privacy and to be near fellow-cubist painter Georges Braque, the couple decided to rent a villa in Sorgues.

### SPECIFIC SITES IN SORGUES

**21 Ruelle des Écoles.**   This villa was rented by Picasso and Eva in the summer of 1912. While here he produced many cubist paintings including "Man with a Guitar" and "The Artist's Model." Before leaving in October he removed some wallpaper and painted a large still-life mural, "Ma Jolie." His friend Georges Braque, who had once earned his living as a house painter, paid the owner 15 francs, replaced the wall and brought the painting to Picasso in Paris in good condition. Today the house is barely visible behind the high garden wall and another villa (21 bis) that has been built at the front of the property. However, there is a plaque denoting Picasso's stay here.

**471 Route d'Entraigues.**   This was the villa rented by Georges Braque and his wife from 1912–1916, although he was in military service for part of this time. During the summer of 1912, when Picasso was living here with Eva, the two cubist painters continued their close working relationship which they had established in Paris. There is a history plaque outside the house denoting Braque's stay. However, the house next door at 481 is named "Bel Air" which is the name of the villa given in Braque biographies.

## Antibes / Juan-les-Pins

Antibes and Juan-les-Pins are located on the Cap d'Antibes which lies between Cannes and Nice. The city of Antibes received its name from the

Greeks around 400 B.C. as a protected cove "opposite" Corsica. This was the first place on the Côte d'Azur that Picasso settled for a lengthy stay. He had spent many vacations on the Cap from as early as 1920 and in 1935 had bought a small house here for his mistress, Marie-Thérèse Walter. He also stayed in Antibes for the summer of 1939. During World War II he had remained in Paris almost all of the time but at the war's end he again traveled to the South. At this time, when Picasso was looking for a large studio in the area in which to work, he met a local Antibes scholar, Romuald Dor de la Souchère, who was in the process of converting the ancient castle of the Grimaldi family into a municipal museum. This fortuitous meeting led to the town's allowing the artist to live and work in part of the castle, which has since become a fine museum dedicated to his work.

### SPECIFIC SITES IN ANTIBES / JUAN-LES-PINS

**Villa La Vigie, at end of Chemin de La Vigie.**    This lovely villa, with a view of the sea, was a summer retreat for Picasso during the 1920s. While here he executed many paintings with a bathing theme influenced by classical Greek art. The villa still stands in its large garden; the small street is accessible from Impasse du Tanagra off Chemin de Saint Jean, north of RN-7.

**Hôtel du Cap d'Antibes, Boulevard John F. Kennedy.**    This posh hotel,

*Hotel du Cap d'Antibes where Picasso stayed in 1923*

opened in February, 1870, is located on a large estate at the southwest end
of Cap d'Antibes. One of Picasso's early stays in the area was spent here
with his wife, Olga, in 1923. At that time the couple's friends, Gerald and
Sara Murphy, were also guests here. Some believe that Picasso was infatuated with this American socialite and may have had an affair with her
while here, especially since her husband left Antibes to spend part of this
summer in Venice with Cole Porter. One scholar believes that hundreds of
paintings and drawings from this period were inspired by Picasso's feelings for Sara. These works primarily feature large idealized females that
are at least partially nude, such as "Woman in White," which is in the
Metropolitan Museum of Art in New York. The hotel is still the epitome
of the luxurious Riviera lifestyle and continues to boast an impressive list
of celebrated guests.

✦ **Villa Ste-Geneviève, Avenue du Docteur Hochet (close to the sea).**    In the
1930s, when having severe marital problems, Picasso used this villa as a
retreat. Today only three villas are left on the street, none with this name.
If it still stands it is no longer known as Villa Ste-Geneviève.

**Palais Albert I, 44 Boulevard Albert I.**    During the summer of 1939
Picasso and his mistress, Dora Maar, had an apartment in this lovely 1928
art-deco building. This stay was aborted by the outbreak of World War II.
The couple hurried to Paris to assess the safety of their belongings there
and then left the capital to spend the remainder of the summer in Royan.

**Place du Général de Gaulle (formerly Place Victor Massé).**    Although this
lovely square is now quite modern, in 1939 it had a number of cafés which
were frequented by Picasso during his stay here. This was reminiscent of
his life in Paris.

**Seaside Promenade.**    During the summer of 1939 Picasso and Dora often
walked along this promenade at night. The artist was fascinated by the
many fishermen with their lanterns and used this as the subject of a major
painting. Today "Fishing by Night at Antibes" is in the Museum of
Modern Art in New York.

★ **Musée Picasso, Château d'Antibes, Place Mariejol.**    This 12th-century
castle was built on the foundations of a Roman camp with the ancient
stones from that structure. The ruined edifice was purchased by the town
in 1925 to house a municipal museum. In the mid-1940s, Picasso lived
and worked here for over six months and produced a remarkable number
of works including twenty-five colossal canvases. When he left, Picasso
donated everything he had done during this period to the fledgling museum. This gift consisted of one hundred eighty-one paintings and drawings which depicted the joy and fantasy inspired by the beauty and myth-
ology of the Mediterranean Sea which lay beneath the windows of the

*Picasso Museum, Antibes*

château. Picasso later donated to the museum seventy-six pieces of ceramics that he had crafted in nearby Vallauris. With these gifts this museum became the first in the world devoted to his work, predating those in Barcelona and Paris.

## Vallauris

Pablo Picasso discovered the small ancient town of Vallauris in 1936 while summering in nearby Mougins. Located in the hills six kilometers northeast of Cannes, Vallauris has a tradition in the craft of ceramics which dates from Roman times. Although this industry was in severe decline at the end of World War II, it was destined to be revived due to a casual visit by Picasso in 1946. During a day in the town, the sixty-five-year-old artist dropped in at the Madoura Pottery studio, one of the last remaining in operation at that time. He was invited to try his hand at this craft which he had always admired as a combination of painting, sculpture and drawing. The natural facility with which he created a piece of pottery impressed both him and his hosts, Georges and Suzanne Ramié, and he began returning frequently to work at their studio. Picasso's presence revitalized the entire ceramics industry here and the town became the center of his work during the last three decades of his life. Vallauris was also chosen by him in 1958 as the site of the public unveiling of his 120-square-yard panel, "The Fall of Icarus," which he had painted for the UNESCO building in Paris.

### SPECIFIC SITES IN VALLAURIS

★ **Madoura Pottery, Avenue des Anciens Combats d'A. F. N.**   In 1946 Picasso began working here on ceramics; during the next year alone he completed over two hundred works. His production here continued for over twenty-five years. Today this establishment is a combination of an active pottery studio adjoined by a gallery which displays many of Picasso's creations along with those of contemporary artists. Also on display are some mementos of his work here. The business, located just off Avenue Georges-Clemenceau, is still run by a member of the Ramié family.

**Madoura Boutique, Avenue Georges-Clemenceau and Avenue du Tapis Vert.**   This boutique, also under the direction of the Ramié family, is the exclusive outlet for the sale of reproductions of Picasso's ceramic creations during his twenty-five years of work at the Madoura Pottery studio. The shop is decorated with many photographs of Picasso at work in the studio.

**La Galloise, 515 Chemin Lintier.**   In 1948 Picasso bought this villa in Vallauris and settled here with his mistress Françoise Gilot and their year-old son, Claude. The following year the couple had a daughter, Paloma. The small privately-owned villa, away from the town center, was the home of Picasso and his family until 1953. These happy times were then marred when his relationship with Françoise ended.

**Place Isnard.**   In this square, near the Château Musée, stands Picasso's larger-than-life bronze sculpture, "Man with a Lamb," which he presented to the town in 1950 on the occasion of his being made an honorary citizen. At this time he requested that the statue be installed so that children could play around it and the authorities complied with his wishes.

*Exterior of the Madoura Pottery Studio, Vallauris*

*Interior of the Madoura Pottery Studio, Vallauris*

*Picasso's bronze sculpture "Man with a Lamb"*
*in Place Isnard, Vallauris*

★ **Musée Picasso, Place de la Libération.** In 1951 Picasso was honored with a celebration of his seventieth birthday in the surviving 13th-century chapel of the town's ancient priory. He was greatly impressed by the church's interior, especially the vaulting, and requested permission to decorate its walls with two large painted panels. The municipal authorities enthusiastically accepted his idea and made available to him an old perfumery which was large enough to accommodate the project. In 1953 the works, entitled "War" and "Peace," were installed in the chapel which has been a national museum since 1959. The murals, which cover over 100 square meters, are considered one of his finest masterpieces. The two main works are joined by a central panel depicting the desire for peace among the nations of the world. Many of his ceramic works are on display in the outer hallway.

★ **Musée Municipal d'Art Moderne et Contemporain, Place de la Libération.** This museum is housed in a 16th-century Renaissance castle built on the site of the old 12th-century priory. Among the exhibitions of modern and contemporary art are several rooms devoted to Picasso. Many of the ceramics which he made in the nearby Madoura Pottery studio are on display along with some photographs of his years there. In addition, there is a room displaying a number of Picasso lithographs and the original press on which they were printed.

**Perfumery / Studio, 95 Avenue Pablo Picasso (formerly Rue de Fournas).** This building, located between two ceramics manufacturers, once housed the studio in which Picasso worked on the "War" and "Peace" murals. The town eventually gave him possession of the building, a former perfumery, and it was later remodeled into an attractive villa. At the time of our visit it was inhabited by his daughter, Maya.

*Printing press used for Picasso lithographs, Municipal Museum, Vallauris*

*"Hands of Picasso" bread at the Boulangerie Bianco, Vallauris*

✧ **Arena, Place J. Cavasse.** In the early 1950s Picasso successfully used his influence to initiate Spanish-style bullfighting in the town's old arena which was then located in this square. Picasso attended enthusiastically and on one occasion Françoise even led the procession into the bullring. The area is now a parking lot in front of the new town hall.

**17 bis Rue Hoche.** In 1953 this building was the site of the 4th Exposition of Midi Painting, in which Picasso took part along with Fernand Léger, Édouard Pignon and other painters of the region.

**Boulangerie Bianco, 61 Avenue Georges-Clemenceau.** This bakery created a special bread in honor of Pablo Picasso. It is shaped like a large hand with each finger a miniature loaf. Each summer the traditional "Hands of Picasso" are still produced for the pleasure of the locals and the tourists. On the outer wall of the shop is a photo of the artist with one of these loaves. This entire thoroughfare is now the location of many ceramics shops which owe their existence to Picasso's revival of this local craft for which the town has again become famous.

**Bibliothèque Municipal, Place de la Libération.** Shortly after his break-up with Françoise, Picasso took an interest in Jacqueline Roque, a twenty-seven-year-old cousin of the Ramiés who worked at their ceramics studio. In 1955 he and his young companion began living in a sumptuous villa in nearby Cannes, but he continued to work at the Madoura Pottery studio.

*Exterior of Hotel Muscadins, Mougins*

*Interior of Hotel Muscadins, Mougins*

In the Vallauris town hall, which is now the city's library, Picasso married her on March 2, 1961, in his 80th year.

## Mougins

The town of Mougins has a charming hilltop location north of Cannes and still retains part of its 15th-century ramparts. At 700 meters, it is the highest of the "perched" villages on the Côte d'Azur. During the 1930s Picasso stayed in this picturesque village several times. From here he had his chauffeur drive him to Cimiez to visit Henri Matisse. At this time he told his friend Paul Eluard that someday he would live here. More than two decades later he did choose the town for his final home when he began to dislike the over-development of Cannes.

### SPECIFIC SITES IN MOUGINS

**Hôtel Muscadins, 18 Boulevard Georges-Courteline.**   This hotel, formerly called Hôtel Vaste Horizon, was the summer residence of Picasso in 1936, 1938 and 1939, when he visited here with his poet-friend Paul Eluard. He occupied the only room with a balcony and shared it with a monkey which he had acquired from a local pet shop. Although Picasso was extremely fond of these animals, considering them as caricatures of human beings, he did return the monkey to the shop when it bit him. Also while staying here Picasso was joined by Dora Maar, who would become his mistress from 1936 to 1945. It was at this hotel, during a 1961 visit with Jacqueline, that he decided to look for a home in Mougins and in celebration of that decision he proposed marriage to her. In 1985 the four-star hotel was renovated but still has only one room with a balcony.

**La Mas Notre-Dame-de-Vie, Chemin de la Chapelle.**   This house, which overlooks the 17th-century chapel of Notre-Dame-de-Vie, was purchased by Picasso in 1961 and was his principal home after 1965. In 1973 he died here in his studio, still at work at age 91. Today the unmarked house, a private residence, is difficult to see because of the many high shrubs that surround it.

★ **Musée de la Photographie, Porte Sarrazine.**   This museum, located in one of the town's old gates, houses a collection of over one hundred photographs depicting the last two decades of Picasso's life in the Côte d'Azur area. They include pictures of his homes in Antibes, Cannes and Mougins and of memorabilia such as his palette and his rocking chair. There are also many photos of the artist with family members and friends at work and at play.

*La Mas Notre-Dame-de-Vie, Mougins, Picasso's last residence*

*Garden of La Mas Notre-Dame-de-Vie, Mougins*

## St-Paul-de-Vence

This fortified medieval town, which lies in the hills west of Nice, was discovered by artists in the 1920s and its narrow streets have since become crowded with galleries and tourists as well as the many artists who live and work there. At the west end of the village is the **Auberge de la Colombe d'Or**, a fashionable hotel and restaurant which was opened by Paul Roux and his wife, Titine, as a café shortly after World War I. During its early days as an inn the owner often indulged his love for art by allow-

*Auberge de la Colombe d'Or, St-Paul-de-Vence*

ing struggling artists to pay for their room and board with paintings. Today the hotel owns an excellent collection of art which includes work by Picasso as well as Marc Chagall, Henri Matisse, Joan Miró and others. Also, in the lobby to the right of the desk, there is a photograph of Picasso who often came here for dinner on his way home from visiting Matisse in Nice.

## Nice / Cimiez

Nice was founded by the Greeks of Marseille in the 4th century B.C. but remained a small trading post for many centuries. Cimiez was established as a Roman colony which was later destroyed by the barbarians in the 8th century. The Counts of Provence began to redevelop Nice in the 10th century and that has now become the larger of the two. Its spectacular location on a lovely bay of the Mediterranean Sea makes Nice one of the most popular resorts of the French Riviera while Cimiez retains its quiet residential atmosphere in the hills just above the city. Henri Matisse, a friend and rival of Picasso, was in the habit of traveling in southern climes during the winter and discovered Nice in 1917. He made the area his primary home for the rest of his life and Picasso often visited him at his Cimiez residence. Nice was the venue for the production of a film on Picasso's life done in 1956.

### SPECIFIC SITES IN NICE / CIMIEZ

**Hôtel Regina, Avenue Regina.** This large elaborate building, located at the corner of Avenue Regina and Avenue de Cimiez, just at the upper end of the Boulevard de Cimiez, was built in 1897 to accommodate Queen Victoria and the English colony in Nice. In 1938 Matisse bought two third-floor apartments. He remained here until his death in 1954, except for some years during the war when he moved to the safer area of Vence in the nearby hills. From the 1930s until Matisse's death Picasso often visited the older artist here. While living in nearby Vallauris he did so every two weeks. The vast rooms of Matisse's apartment were full of fabrics, hangings, plants and other objects which expressed the colorful taste of the artist. Among these were over three hundred tropical birds which he had begun to acquire after his trip to Tahiti in 1930. A memento of this trip was a colorful larger-than-life wooden sculpture of an idol from New Guinea. On one of the many visits which Picasso made here Matisse presented this monstrosity to his guest, saying that is was appropriate to his personality. Picasso, who preferred to think he was more suited to some elegant art piece from China, was very unhappy about this gift and postponed sending for it as he had promised. After much waiting Matisse fi-

*Hotel Regina, Cimiez, where Picasso often visited
Henri Matisse*

nally had it delivered to him at Vallauris; Picasso felt obliged to keep it and soon grew to like it. Today it is prominently displayed in the Picasso Museum in Paris!

**Atelier La Victorine, 16 Avenue Edouard Grinda.**   In the summer of 1956 Picasso came frequently to this studio, at the west end of the city, to participate in the making of Georges Clouzot's film "Le Mystère Picasso," which was based on his life. The studio, located on extensive premises, is still in operation.

✧**Galerie H. Matarasso, 36 Boulevard Dubouchage.**   This was the site of an exhibition entitled "Picasso: a Half-Century of Illustrated Books" held in December, 1956. The gallery is no longer there.

**Musée Matisse, 164 Avenue des Arènes de Cimiez.**   The impressive collection of this museum, which is devoted mainly to the work of Henri Matisse, includes some ceramic works by Picasso. During his lifetime Picasso considered Matisse as the only artist in his own class.

**Galerie du Château, 14 Rue Droite.**   The collection of this gallery, located in the old part of Nice, has 200 Picasso works.

## *Fréjus*

Fréjus, founded by Julius Caesar in 49 B.C., lies on the Mediterranean coast to the southwest of Cannes. Like Arles, it is rich in Roman monuments, including the oldest arena in France. It was in this **Arena** that Picasso attended bullfights in 1939 with his Catalan friend and secretary, Jaime Sabartés. This trip was made from Paris to help him recover from his grief at the death of his friend and associate, art dealer Ambroise Vollard. Later, in 1961, he was involved with André Malraux in a campaign to raise funds to restore this city after it had been partially destroyed by a bursting dam. Picasso donated many of his works for this cause. He returned for more bullfights in 1963 with his new wife, Jacqueline.

## *Ménerbes*

This small Provençal village, which juts out of the north face of the Luberon, lies about thirty kilometers southeast of Avignon. It is dominated by an impressive citadel from the 13th century. Picasso lived here for two brief periods early in his southern years. In the fall of 1945, when he was changing mistresses from Dora Maar to Françoise Gilot, he bartered a painting for a house on **Rue du Portail Neuf** which he gave to Dora as a final gesture. The large house, located in the center of the old village near the Mairie, had once belonged to one of Napoleon's generals. The façade was stark except for twenty windows covered with shutters and a handsome portal. This part of the town was called the "cold coast" by the local folks and running water was available on only one of the structure's four floors. In 1946 the 65-year-old Picasso spent some time here with Françoise during which she conceived their first child. He was quite amused that this should have occurred in the house borrowed from his previous mistress. While here Picasso and Françoise often ate at a local restaurant, Café de l'Union. The village has changed little since that time and is well worth a visit.

## Villefranche-sur-Mer

This fishing port and resort town lies on the coast at the head of Rade de Villefranche just between Nice and Cap Ferrat. Picasso's connection to this village is derived through two friends of his, Henri Goetz and Jean Cocteau.

### SPECIFIC SITES IN VILLEFRANCHE-SUR-MER

**38 Rue Baron de Bres.** This house, in the old section of the town, was the home of Picasso's friends Henri Goetz and his wife Christine Boumeester. Picasso inspired these artists to work on ceramics with him at Vallauris.

**Musée Goetz-Boumeester, Fosse de La Citadelle.** This small museum is located in the complex of the town's 16th-century citadel. Its collection is dedicated to the lives and work of Henri Goetz and his wife, Christine Boumeester, who were friends of Pablo Picasso. Among the items on display are a pastel done by Picasso and inscribed by him to his friends in 1958, one photo of him on the beach with the couple in 1947 and another of him and Goetz at Vallauris where they worked together on ceramics. In the entrance foyer of the museum is "The Great Sorcerer," a large drawing by another of their friends, Joan Miró.

**Chapelle St-Pierre, Quai Amiral-Courbet.** In 1957 this ancient fishermen's chapel was totally redecorated by Jean Cocteau with murals based on the life of St. Peter. It is certain that Picasso came here to see this major work of his lifelong friend.

## St-Tropez

This ancient seaport sits peacefully on the remote side of the Gulf of St-Tropez. Its old Provençal atmosphere and narrow streets make the village one of the favorite spots on the Côte d'Azur. In the 19th-century Renaissance-style **Mairie**, on Rue de la Mairie, Picasso and his mistress, Françoise Gilot, were witnesses at the marriage of his close friend Paul Eluard in June, 1951.

## Montpellier

Montpellier is the capital of the province of Bas Languedoc and has an impressive history which dates from medieval times. Its location ten kilometers from the Mediterranean coast was an important stop for traders of spices and pilgrims to Santiago de Compostella in Spain and since the 13th century it has been the site of a major university and medical school. This city remains one of the most charming in the South of France and boasts one of the country's finest provincial art museums, the **Musée Fabre**. Among the many masterpieces of the collection is Eugène Delacroix's "Women of Algiers" which Picasso used as one of the models for his 1954–1955 series of abstract paintings on this theme. In preparation for this work, Picasso visited the museum which is located on Boulevard Sarrail.

## Cannes

Cannes's development as a resort began by chance in 1834 when a prominent English visitor was forced to stay there on his way to Nice due to an outbreak of cholera in the larger city. At the time Cannes was a small fishing village of four thousand inhabitants but the beauty of its location prompted the gentleman to build a home there. This was his holiday residence for the rest of his life and his example brought many other sun-seeking English families to the site. Today it rivals Nice as a resort, confer-

*Picasso's villa La Californie, Cannes*

*Palm Beach Casino, Cannes, where Picasso's wedding reception was held in 1961*

ence setting and festival locale. In 1955, after his breakup with long-term mistress Françoise Gilot, Picasso bought a luxurious villa here and moved from nearby Vallauris with his new partner, Jacqueline Roque. This purchase was another major step in his removal from the Paris world to that of the South. He had recently had his ex-wife, Olga, buried in this city and would later celebrate his second marriage here. It was also in Cannes that the artist met film director Georges-Henri Clouzot with whom he later collaborated on a film about his own life, "Le Mystère Picasso," which debuted at the 1957 Cannes Film Festival.

### SPECIFIC SITES IN CANNES

**Hôtel Martinez, 73 Boulevard de la Croisette.**   In 1952, before obtaining the old perfumery from the town of Vallauris, Picasso began work on his large panels of "War" and "Peace" in one of the halls of this luxury hotel which is still operating on the sea front of Cannes.

**La Californie (now called Pavillon de Flore), 22 Avenue de Coste Belle.** This luxurious villa, set in the hills of Cannes overlooking the sea, was bought by Picasso in 1955. He lived here with Jacqueline for much of the time between this purchase and 1965, with some interludes at other villas which he began to accumulate during these affluent years. At this home he installed a dovecote for his beloved pigeons. Picasso also had a large studio here and greatly loved the lighting in the house. It was here that he painted his 120-square-yard panel for the UNESCO building in Paris in 1956. Today the lovely home belongs to his granddaughter, Flore.

**Palm Beach Casino, La Croisette.**   This elegant casino is located at the tip of La Croisette, a small peninsula which forms the east coast of the Bay of Cannes. It was here that the reception for the wedding of Pablo Picasso and Jacqueline Roque was held on March 2, 1961.

## Menton

Menton, the warmest spot on the Riviera, is located near the Italian border. This city was for a long time part of Monaco and alternated between French and Sardinian control until becoming part of France in 1860. Like Cannes and Nice it has been a popular resort for over one hundred years. The major connection of this city to Picasso is his lifelong friendship and working relationship with writer/artist Jean Cocteau.

### SPECIFIC SITES IN MENTON

**Musée Jean-Cocteau, Bastion du Port.**   This museum, located in a restored 17th-century seaside fortress, is dedicated to Jean Cocteau who oversaw its establishment. Much of the collection consists of artistic works donated by Cocteau's friends in his honor. Picasso's contribution was a pencil portrait of Cocteau done in 1916, the year they met. A display of postcards includes several exchanged between the two over the years. Two of the books exhibited also are related to Picasso: the first, *Le Coq et L'Arlequin* (1918) has a portrait of Cocteau and two monograms by Picasso; the other is a 1926 collection of Cocteau essays, including one entitled "Picasso."

**Salle des Mariages, Mairie, Rue de la République.**   This hall, where marriages are still performed, was decorated with impressive murals by Cocteau during 1957–1958. The room is a celebrated work and certainly must have been visited by Picasso, his intimate friend.

**Musée des Beaux-Arts, 3 Avenue de la Madone.**   This municipal art museum is housed in the Palais Carnoles, the ancient summer residence of the Princes of Monaco. The excellent collection is complemented by an extensive sculpture garden which includes a bronze bust of Picasso by Bruno Tripodi nestled under the orange trees. There are also two sculptures of Jean Cocteau.

## Arles

The Rhone River port of Arles was founded by the Greeks in 6 B.C. and later taken over by the Romans under Julius Caesar when it prospered as a major site on the main road between Rome and Spain. Its importance declined during medieval times when it was part of the country of Provence and the power was shifted to Aix-en-Provence. Today it has revived mainly due to tourism attracted by the many vestiges of Roman civilization and the settings of many of the paintings by Vincent van Gogh. Arles is one of the places where Picasso went to attend bullfights. The love of this sport had been instilled in him as a child in Spain and remained with him throughout his long life. In 1970 Arles awarded him the "Freedom of the City" and he subsequently donated to the city fifty-seven drawings.

### SPECIFIC SITES IN ARLES

**Les Arènes, Rond-Point des Arènes.**   This marvelous amphitheater, one of the many Roman monuments to be found in the city, dates from the 1st century A.D. It originally had a capacity of twenty-six thousand spectators. Among the many contemporary uses of the arena is the staging of bullfights. In 1956, and again in 1963, Picasso enjoyed his favorite sport here from a front-row seat in the shade.

**Musée Réattu, Rue du Grand-Prieuré.**   This museum, on the banks of the Rhone River, is housed in the 15th-century mansion which once belonged to the local painter Jacques Réattu. Among the museum's holdings are fifty-seven drawings from early 1971 which were given to the city by Picasso just two years before his death. In addition, the collection also has Picasso's lovely 1923 portrait of his mother, done in realistic style at Cap d'Antibes and an abstract portrait of Lee Miller as an Arlesienne, painted in Mougins in 1937.

## Nîmes

The ancient city of Nîmes boasts many interesting structures from Roman times. One of the most impressive of these monuments is the two-thousand-year-old **Les Arènes**, which once seated over 20,000 spectators and could be evacuated in five minutes because of the numerous internal stairways, galleries and gates around its large perimeter. Today this centrally-located arena is frequently used for concerts, circuses and both Spanish- and Provençal-style bullfights. In 1963 it was another of the places where Picasso sat in the first row of the shade to watch his favorite sport.

*Château de Vauvenargues where Picasso is buried*

## *Vauvenargues*

This small village lies just to the east of Aix-en-Provence. Its 16th-century château, which stands isolated at the west end of the town, had been owned by the Vauvenargues family from 1790 until 1947. At that time an antiques dealer purchased it and sold all the furnishings. In 1958 Picasso purchased the **Château** and lived there from 1959 to 1961. One of the deciding factors of the deal was the château's view of Mount Ste-Victoire, the mountain immortalized in many paintings of Paul Cézanne whom Picasso greatly admired. Unfortunately, after living here he discovered that the castle was too easily accessible to the public from nearby Aix-en-Provence and he moved back to his villa in Cannes. He did, however, select the garden of the castle as his burial place. After his death, Jacqueline moved back to Vauvenargues and had his 1933 sculpture, "Woman with Vase," placed on his grave. In 1986, thirteen years after his death, she killed herself here on the bed she had shared with Pablo. Their joint gravesite overlooks the peaceful valley of the Infernet River and the majestic peak of Mount Ste-Victoire. Today the castle is privately owned by someone who is obviously not fond of Picasso fans. The closed gates are guarded by unfriendly dogs and a sign reminds visitors that the Picasso museum is in Paris!

# CHAPTER EIGHT

# Other French Cities

Dᴜʀɪɴɢ ʜɪs long life Picasso made extended stays in some French cities outside of the areas covered in the previous chapters. These cities have been grouped here rather than omitting them from the book.

## *Biarritz*

This attractive resort city, once considered the Monte Carlo of the Atlantic coast, lies about twenty-five kilometers from the Spanish border. It was the destination of choice for the rich and famous before the popularity of the Riviera and the home of many wealthy Russian exiles after World War I. Today there is still an impressive Russian Orthodox church here on Rue de l'Impératrice just opposite the opulent Hôtel du Palais. In July, 1918, Picasso and his Russian bride, ballerina Olga Koklova, were invited to spend their honeymoon at La Mimosercue, the Biarritz villa of Madame Eugenia Erranzuriz, a rich Chilean that he had met in Paris a few years before. Afterward, in Paris, Madame Erranzuriz sponsored the Picassos into the right social circles. This caused much annoyance to Gertrude Stein who felt that the artist had been "stolen" from her artistic group.

In the villa where he stayed Picasso painted a mural of two female nudes framing a verse from *Les Saisons* by his dear friend Guillaume Apollinaire. This house was located on Rue de Constantine but unfortunately was demolished in 1964. Picasso also did at least two other paintings while here. One was a painting of girl bathers with the **Biarritz lighthouse** in the background. The other was a portrait of the wife of Paul Rosenberg, a Parisian art dealer who had a villa nearby and whom Picasso first met at this time. Madame Rosenberg was supposedly displeased with his portrayal of her in the portrait and complained that she would rather have been painted by the fashionable Italian portraitist of the time in Paris, Giovanni Boldini. Upon hearing this, Picasso took a new canvas and, in just a few minutes time, presented her with an image of herself in the style of that artist and

*Beach at Biarritz where Picasso spent his honeymoon in 1918*

signed "Boldini." This stay at Biarritz was for the artist a reunification with the sea that he had so enjoyed as a child in Spain. He subsequently began a series of visits to various French coastal cities during the following decade.

## *Fontainebleau*

This town lies in the center of an ancient royal hunting ground of 50,000 acres of forest about sixty kilometers south of Paris. It is the site of the fabulous 16th-century Renaissance palace which was created by François I from the original 12th-century château and in which Napoleon lived for most of his reign. In the spring of 1921, because they had a newborn child, the Picassos decided to spend the summer nearer to Paris. They rented a villa at **33 Boulevard Maréchal Leclerc** (formerly Boulevard Gambetta) in Fontainebleau and stayed there for five months, from May through September. This was a particularly happy period in the life of the artist and his work here was very prolific. It included over one hundred sketches, many of the inside and outside of the house. Although it is privately owned, we had the opportunity to visit the interior of the house and found that Picasso's rendition of the architectural features is still accurate today.

*Front of Picasso's 1921 residence in Fontainebleau*

*Rear of Picasso's 1921 residence in Fontainebleau*

The most important work done there was his cubist painting "Three Musicians," of which he did two versions; they are today in Philadelphia and New York.


## *Dinard*

Dinard is located in Brittany on the eastern end of the Emerald Coast opposite St-Malo. In the 19th century it was a popular destination for English tourists and still remains an attractive resort with lovely beaches and a casino. Picasso stayed here during the summer of 1922 with his wife and infant son. Their stay was unfortunately shortened by an illness which required Olga's return to Paris for surgery. He returned here during the summer of 1928 with his mistress, Marie-Thérèse, and visited still again in 1929.


### SPECIFIC SITES IN DINARD

**Villa Beauregard, 50 Avenue George V.**   Picasso rented this lovely early-18th-century villa during the summer of 1922 and came here with his wife and his year-old son, Paulo. At that time the garden here was one of the loveliest in the city with two Empire columns flanking the entry gate. Among the many sketches that he made while here, some were of various views from this villa. Interestingly, the house had been inhabited by an amateur photographer, Madame Faber, more than sixty years earlier and some of the photographs that she took here are the same subjects as Picasso's sketches.

**Plage de l'Écluse.**   This expansive beach attracted Picasso with its colorful tents and balloons. During his 1922 stay he drew the small-animal races here which were part of the many-faceted August festival. In 1928 he came here almost daily, painting twenty-eight paintings of the beach in thirty days. Today there are two large placards which each show two of these Dinard works along with a commentary on his stays here. One depicts the 1922 paintings "Family on the Beach" and "Two Women Running on the Beach," while the other shows the 1928 works "Bathers on the Beach" and "Ball Players on the Beach."

**Casino, on the Plage de l'Écluse.**   This was one of three casinos that opened during Picasso's 1928 stay in Dinard. The other two have since disappeared. Picasso attended all the gala openings which included bathing-suit competitions, choosing of Miss France and special shows and dances. These events inspired many of his paintings at this time.

*Plaque commemorating Picasso's 1922 work on Plage de l'Écluse, Dinard*

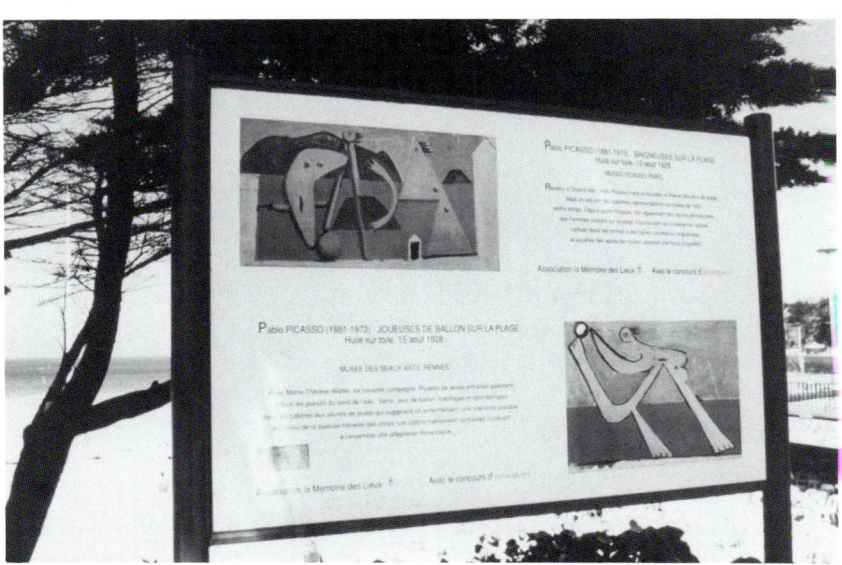

*Plaque commemorating Picasso's 1928 work on Plage de l'Écluse, Dinard*

**Villa Coppinger, 1 Rue Coppinger.**   This late-19th-century mansion was built by a wealthy manufacturer of Cognac. It stands on a bluff above the sea and was the subject of some sketches by Picasso who admired its beauty. After World War II it was subdivided into thirteen apartments but the palatial entry hall remains as the sumptuous lobby of the building.

**Avenue George V.**   This street is lined with many old villas that were here at the time of Picasso's stay. Among the sites on the street that were sketching subjects of his are **Villa La Baie** at #13; **Belle Rive,** an elegant villa with a distinctive square glass dome at #23; the **Public Garden** at #46, which covers the slope between the Avenue George V and the sea; and the **landing place of the St-Malo ferry** at the end of the street.

**Port of St-Servan and the Tour Solidor.**   Still another subject of Picasso's pencil was the port of St-Servan which faces Dinard across the Rance Estuary. His drawings included the formidable 14th-century tower which guards the mouth of this broad waterway.

**Les Roches, 14 Chemin du Tertre Mignon.**   This villa, which has its rear directly on the St-Énogat Beach, was the residence of Picasso and Marie-Thérèse during their 1928 stay in Dinard. The tall and narrow house is located away from the town center in a quiet neighborhood. It is a lovely walk along the sea wall from this beach to the Plage de l'Écluse; one can also continue on to the Pointe de la Vicomte.

**Musée du Site Balnéaire, 12 Rue des Français Libres.**   This municipal museum, located in the restored Villa Eugénie, houses a collection of items dealing with the history of the city. One exhibit is a collection of photographs of celebrated people that have visited Dinard, including Picasso. In a display of bathing fashions from 1880 to 1960 there is a reproduction of one of the colorful beach tents that the artist found attractive and mannequins wearing the apparel seen on his "Bathers." There are several models of the various casinos which were found here during his time as well as some reproductions of his paintings and drawings of Dinard. Finally, there is a display of the photographs of Madame Faber, the 1852–1857 resident of Villa Beauregard whose subjects were very similar to those of Picasso.

## Gisors

This medieval town lies about sixty kilometers southeast of Rouen at the confluence of the rivers Epte, Réveillon and Troesne. Its two great landmarks are its church and its castle. The church of St-Gervais and St-Protais was built in the 13th and 16th centuries. Although heavily damaged when the surrounding area was destroyed in 1940, it is now completely restored.

*Les Roches, Dinard, villa where Picasso lived in 1928*

The castle is a lovely example of 11–12th-century military architecture. The remaining walls and towers now harbor a lovely garden which is freely open to the public. One can also visit the surviving dungeon and towers. In 1931, in the midst of the worldwide depression, Picasso was affluent enough to buy the 17th-century **Château de Boisgeloup**, which is located about two kilometers from the town center. Still married to Olga, the artist wanted this secluded retreat to rendezvous with his mistress, Marie-Thérèse Walter, who would later be the mother of his daughter Maya. The property included a twenty-room mansion on six acres of land and there was also an adjacent carriage house which Picasso converted into a sculpture studio for himself. He used the château as his country home for five years before losing the estate to Olga in their bitter divorce settlement in 1936. It is now the residence of his grandson. To reach the château from Gisors, take the Rue de la Libération (RD-15 bis), toward Paris. Following signs to Boisgeloup, turn right onto Rue du Calvaire and then left onto Rue Pablo Picasso. The château is on the right, a little less than one kilometer from the highway.

## Le Tremblay

The village of Le Tremblay is located about twenty kilometers west of Versailles. In 1936 the Parisian art dealer Ambroise Vollard owned a house here at **13 Grande Rue**, which he intended to use as a location for an artists' colony. At that time Picasso's life was in turmoil. He had lost his Château de Boisgeloup to Olga in a divorce settlement that left his finances in disarray. Out of desperation, he had sent for his friend, Jaime Sabartés, to come from Barcelona to take over the management of his affairs as his secretary. Still entangled in his affair with Marie-Thérèse Walter, who had recently borne him a daughter, he was also involved with a new mistress, Dora Maar. Vollard offered him temporary escape from these complications by putting this house at his disposal. Picasso used it as a residence for Marie-Thérèse and the infant Maya and set up his sculpture studio in the adjacent barn. Dora remained in a Paris apartment to which he frequently shuttled. The town may be reached from Versailles via RN-10 to D-13, which runs directly into the village.

## Royan

This still-popular resort lies on the Atlantic coast just north of Bordeaux. Even prior to its destruction in 1944 it was a fashionable holiday destination for the middle classes. The post-war rebuilding of the city included

*Château de Boisgeloup, Gisors, Picasso residence in 1930s*

the construction of the unique church of Notre-Dame, a reinforced concrete edifice shaped like a huge ship and whose spire towers eighty meters above its surroundings. When World War II began, Picasso and Dora Maar were summering in Antibes but hurried to Paris to assess the safety of their belongings there. They then left the capital and fled here to Royan, some five hundred kilometers to the southwest. After a brief stay he was forced to return to Paris again to secure documentation necessary for resident aliens. Finally, he settled in this coastal town for almost a year, even after the Germans occupied the city in May, 1940. In August of that year

*Marina at Royan*

he went back to Paris, where he remained for the duration of the war. Unfortunately, because of the Allied bombing of the city in 1944, most of the places connected with Picasso's year here no longer exist. We list them below only for the information of those who choose to visit this locale.

### SPECIFIC SITES IN ROYAN

✧ **14 Boulevard Georges-Clemenceau.** This building, now Résidence Le Tigre, is on the site of the 1939 Hôtel du Tigre where Picasso stayed when he first arrived in the city after the outbreak of World War II. A short time later, when he returned with his proper papers, he rented a studio in the upper story of the nearby Villa Gerbier de Jones on the corner of Boulevard Albert I and Avenue Bel Aire, which has since been renamed Boulevard Franck Lamy for a local resistance fighter. While he was living there, sometimes with a new mistress, Dora Maar stayed at this hotel when she later joined him.

✧ **Les Voilière, near the harbor.** In December, 1939, Picasso moved to this building in which he had a top-floor studio with three large windows facing the water. Here he painted one of his many portraits of his friend and secretary, Jaime Sabartés, who accompanied him here. This painting is now in the Picasso Museum in Paris. He and Sabartés liked to walk on the nearby **Quai du Bac** and sit on a bench facing the harbor. The area is now entirely rebuilt including the large modern premises where the freshly caught fish is auctioned. On this site Picasso painted the traditional fish market that was its precursor.

**Café Le Régent, 12 Front de Mer.**   This café, although modernized, is still operating. During his stay in Royan, Picasso frequented this establishment and found out the news of the war here. A 1940 painting of this "Café de Royan" is now in the Picasso Museum in Paris.

**Le Marché Central, Rue Henri-Meriot.**   This modern market building, shaped like a parachute, replaced another which was destroyed by bombs. It houses the same colorful bazaar that Picasso frequented while living in Royan. He loved to comb such places for unusual objects which he would use as painting subjects or as parts of sculptures.

# Bibliography

Cabanne, Pierre. *Le Siècle de Picasso*. 2 volumes. Paris: Denoël, 1975.

Daix, Pierre. *Picasso*. New York: Frederick A. Praeger Publishers, 1965.

Gedo, Mary Mathews. *Picasso: Art as Autobiography*. Chicago: University of Chicago Press, c1980.

Gilot, Françoise and Lake, Carlton. *Life with Picasso*. New York: McGraw-Hill Book Co., 1964.

Gilot, Françoise. *Matisse and Picasso: A Friendship in Art*. New York: Doubleday, c1990.

Haight, Mary Ellen Jordan, and Haight, James Jordan. *Walks in Picasso's Barcelona*. Salt Lake City: Gibbs-Smith Publisher, [1992].

Hierholtz, Roseline. "Picasso et Fontainebleau." *Notre Départment: La Seine-et-Marne* No. 2 (Août–Septembre 1988): 48.

Huffington, Arianna Stassinopoulos. *Picasso: Creator and Destroyer*. New York: Simon & Schuster, 1988.

Kimmelman, Michael. "A Secret Picasso Muse: Jazz-Age Luminary Linked to Paintings." *International Herald Tribune*, 23–24 April 1994, p. 6.

Levy, Lorraine. *Picasso*. New York: Henry Holt & Co., 1990.

Lord, James. *Picasso & Dora: a personal memoir*. New York: Fromm International, 1993.

McCully, Marilyn. "Picasso and the Catalan Colony in Paris before the Great War." In *Paris: Center of Artistic Enlightenment*, edited by George Mauner, et al. Papers in Art History from The Pennsylvania State University, vol IV. University Park, Pennsylvania: The Pennsylvania State University, c1988.

Mac Gregor-Hastie, Roy. *Picasso's Women*. London: Lennard Publishers, 1988.

O'Brian, Patrick. *Picasso*. New York: G. P. Putnam's Sons, 1976.

Padin, Angel. *Los Cincos Años Coruñeses de Pablo Ruiz Picasso (1891–1895)*. Coruña, Spain: Excma. Diputación Provincial de a Coruña, 1991.

Penrose, Roland. *Picasso: his Life and Work*. New York: Harper and Brothers Publishers, 1959.

Penrose, Roland. *Portrait of Picasso*. New York: The Metropolitan Museum of Art, 1957.

Picasso, Pablo. *Pablo Picasso: a Retrospective*. Edited by William Rubin. New York: The Museum of Modern Art, c1980.

Sabartés, Jaime. *Picasso: an Intimate Portrait*. New York: Prentice-Hall, Inc., 1948.

Wertenbaker, Lael, and The Editors of Time-Life Books. *The World of Picasso, 1881–1973*. Revised ed. Alexandria, Va.: Time-Life Books, 1980.